WORK &

DIVORCE

VOCATIONAL EVALUATION IN FAMILY LAW

Betty Kohlenberg

Work and Divorce: Vocational Evaluation in Family Law

Betty Kohlenberg

ISBN: 978-0-9855538-2-1

Available from:

Kohlenberg & Associates Vocational Counseling Services
San Francisco CA
(415) 665-6902   www .bkohlenberg.com

Table of Contents

ACKNOWLEDGMENTS

So many people gave time and attention to help in the creation of this book, my gratitude grows daily. My wonderful and skilled editor Judy Knipe made sense of my initial drafts – and of so much else. The Bay Area Vocational Experts group – Lisa Trustin, Marlis Bruns, Susan Stevenson, Rob Cottle, Sandra Schuster, Rachel Hawk, Peter Eliaser, and Susan Miller – gave me priceless feedback as they do in all our time together. Patrick McGinnis's organization and sense of humor have buoyed me up. The IARP Forensic Section and its listserve participants have been an invaluable resource, with special thanks to Carl Gann, Ann Wallace and Lynne Tracy.

I want also to thank Nan Reiley, Michael and Debby Smith, Meredith Watts, Mark Misrok, Rosa Hippler, and Joanne Green for insights, encouragement, and guidance, and Diana Brohard and Arikka Johnson for their designers' visions. Thellen Levy, Michael Tobriner, Rodney Johnson, Vivian Holley, Sandra Blair, Garrett Dailey, Peggy Bennington, Pauline Tesler, Marjorie Slabach and many others in the family law community have been wise and instructive colleagues throughout the years.

The evaluees who have shared their stories, fears, desires, goals, and their tears have taught me so much. I am especially grateful for the chance to be part of their work lives.

And to my beloved Toby, Amber, Kaitlyn, and Maya, my joy from their presence in my life can never be overstated.

Their input has been invaluable; any mistakes are my own.

For Philip
1942-2006

Cover photo: Diana Brohard

At first glance, the term *vocational evaluation* seems to describe a formally organized and immutable process. In fact, although there are specific procedures followed in every vocational evaluation, each evaluator practices slightly differently, and the process can be varied to fit the clients who undergo it. Vocational evaluations in family law are evolving, each state has its own laws and precedent-setting cases, and each practitioner uses personally crafted methods that supplement both long-established precedents and those based on newer best practices.

The aim of a vocational evaluation is to form a projection of the client's potential earnings and a plan for vocational activity. My own path to becoming a vocational evaluator was neither planned nor projected. It is true that my 30-plus year-old vocational counseling practice is anchored in my fascination with counseling that has been a part of me since childhood. But vocational counseling includes assessment and planning, and initially I did very little of either in a formal way to transform my counselor instincts into thirty years of counseling services in private practice. Spontaneity, innovation, and opportunities marked the major shifts in my counseling practice. In 1974, if I had asked a vocational counselor what I should do with my life and my newly acquired master's degree in vocational rehabilitation, she would not have been able to suggest the paths I took with that diploma because the profession I practice now did not exist then.

We cannot always see what opportunities will arise. When Mack Sennett's Keystone Film Company offered Charlie Chaplin a film contract to make comedies, he accepted the chance thinking the films would enhance his vaudeville stage career. He did not see how movies would become his career. (Vance, 2010) The contradiction between what I did personally in my vocational life and what I advise for others always makes me laugh. I propose career ideas for clients with the intent that the guidance will be useful, but I know the suggestions may not be what they actually do with their lives, not least because new paths are always opening. My counsel is certainly not a mandate, because peoples' lives are their own to choose.

Strangely, this inconsistency does not make me doubt the usefulness of vocational evaluations. I have tried to describe what I have learned about the process of helping people with careers while they are going through their divorces, and I offer this information to you in the spirit of helpfulness rather than prescription, as a basis for your own spontaneity and creativity.

This book has many potential audiences – family law attorneys and judges, both new and experienced; career counselors and vocational rehabilitation counselors who practice or want to practice as forensic vocational evaluators; and people going through divorce. Although many legal references are from California family law, the principles from this state's laws and cases will inform the practice of vocational evaluations generally. Evaluators in other states will modify their work to conform to the laws in their states. The methodology is applicable nationally.

. . . I do the work I love;

And in it find a rich reward . . .

For few may do the work they love,

That fits them as a hand a glove,

And gives them joy.

Robert Service (1874–1958), *Work and Joy*

CHAPTER ONE – WHAT A VOCATIONAL EVALUATION IS

Love and work are the cornerstones of our humanness.

Sigmund Freud (1856-1939)

THE LINK BETWEEN WORK AND DIVORCE

The word divorce has had a consistent definition since its earliest citation in 1377, and probably was used earlier. After all, people have been joining in marriage unions and leaving them for millennia. Its Latin root *divortium* (OED, 1971) comes from *divertere*, to turn aside, specifically, describing a woman who separates from or leaves her husband. Professor and translator David Bellos (2011) tells us that *divortium* also meant "watershed" or "fork in the road," and these alternate uses of the original term contribute meaningful metaphors for the experience of a divorce. Most people think of their divorces as a watershed time in their lives, a deciding point when a person takes, in Robert Frost's words, a diverging road that makes all the difference.

The word work, on the other hand, requires twenty-eight columns of the Oxford English Dictionary to cover its thirty-nine major definitions. The word stems from the Old English *weork* with its first use citations dating from the tenth century. Originally from the word for action, work has so many uses and describes such a major life activity that one of the first questions Americans ask each other is, "what [work] do you do?" We do not even need to say aloud the word work; doing implies working.

The two concerns of work[1] and divorce touch on the most significant aspects of an adult life: what you do and with whom you connect, that is, work and love. Freud said, according to Erikson, "Love and work, work and love…that's all there is."[2] The primary link between work and divorce starts with work's association with money; division of financial assets is a major marker in the separation of the previously married pair. Both work and divorce carry much more weight in a person's life than that simple equation, however, making discussions and decisions about them some of the most difficult and emotionally fraught experiences we can have.

Not surprisingly, when the question of work arises in the context of divorce, most facets of a couple's lives come under scrutiny. It is a time of many questions, much uncertainty, and a major commitment to reach a resolution.

VOCATIONAL SERVICES IN DIVORCES

Family law attorneys and the divorcing parties, judges, and mediators ask a variety of specialized experts to help them reach divorce settlements or establish credible information for the court's decisions: real estate experts assess property, business evaluators gauge the value of a business or private practice, psychologists and therapists advise about custody arrangements and care of dependent children. Attorneys apply a vocational evaluator's salary data to reach a settlement, just as they use numerical information from a real estate or business evaluation. Similarly, just as custody evaluators help couples work out interpersonal relationships between parents and children, vocational evaluators aid evaluees in developing an effective personal career plan to achieve the positions they want in the work world.

Vocational evaluators clarify a divorcing person's relationship to the world of work not only for attorneys and the courts, but also for the divorcing couple. When a marriage dissolves, the vocational evaluation's primary function is to help the couple (known as "the parties") and their attorneys understand a party's earnings potential. This is used to calculate the amount of money the supporting spouse will give to the supported spouse. A secondary reason, though just as important, is to make vocational counseling services available. The career plan not only guides the evaluee in developing his or her relationship with the work world, it helps the parties project future earnings for long-term support calculations, establishes expectations of costs and duration of any needed training, and sets guidelines for implementing the plan. Vocational evaluators can work with both supported and supporting spouses.

Using a methodology guided by the state's family law statutes, the vocational evaluator uses expertise, advanced training, and specialized knowledge to assess a spouse's present and future vocational position: his or her employability and earning capacity. The vocational evaluator's expert conclusions about the likely outcomes of various career options shape both financial plans in the form of spousal and child support, and personal plans such as career moves, based on individualized, current, and realistic information.

The California Family Law Code contains expectations for vocational evaluation services that extend beyond earnings figures. Written into the law is a clear indication that the evaluation's purpose is not only to supply information to both parties for support calculations, but that the supported party is to be helped to reenter the labor market to generate an income as close as possible to the marital standard of living. The multiple intents for the vocational evaluation process appear in the Family Code's terminology; the mandated qualifications of the expert make clear the skills that the law intends the evaluator to use. See Appendix C, Family Law Code Section 4331(d).

- Vocational evaluations are used to determine spousal support amounts

- Vocational evaluations are used to create career plans

VOCATIONAL EVALUATION GOALS AND COMPONENTS

As a primary goal, an assessment of the spouse's skill, knowledge, abilities, and potential barriers related to employment will meet the legally mandated aims of defining a person's abilities to work, opportunities to work, and work income projections by producing:

- A list of viable job options for which the person is or may become qualified and for which there are opportunities in the labor market

- A set of potential earning ranges associated with those jobs

An integral reason for involving a vocational expert in a family law case is to help the supported spouse decide on a career, since earnings are specifically tied to job titles. If the supported spouse does not have a clearly identified career, the vocational planning is an essential first step in connecting the earnings projections realistically to the individual, rather than being a hypothetical response or a guess. No one enters the job market generically; each worker brings personal values, interests, and skills that shape his or her place in the labor market. This personalized assessment underpins the report's conclusions that list possible job options and a realistic set of measures to reach the vocational goals. This part of the vocational evaluation results in:

- A vocational plan to achieve employment in the chosen field.

For the evaluation to be effective, some services are essential to most if not all cases; others occur as called for in individual situations.

ESSENTIAL VOCATIONAL EVALUATION ELEMENTS

- <u>Earning capacity evaluation</u> will determine the client's skills, abilities, aptitudes, physical and mental capacities, interests and values, and will identify appropriate job titles with associated salary ranges and access to labor market. **Purpose: assess ability to work**.

- <u>Labor market research</u> will collect current information about potential earnings and availability of openings in identified jobs and industries, from published sources and contacts with local employers or information sources. **Purpose: demonstrate opportunity to work**.

- <u>Vocational planning</u> will explain and outline the steps necessary to achieve a vocational goal, comparing sources of training and programs, if useful, and including costs, timing, and identification of potential barriers. **Purpose: assist spouse to take advantage of the opportunity to work to achieve earning capacity.**

SUPPLEMENTAL VOCATIONAL SERVICES

In addition to conducting the Vocational Evaluation Process to determine earning capacity, a vocational expert should be able to:

- Assign and instruct a client in useful activities to assist the evaluation such as:

  - Obtaining transcripts and relevant documentation of education

  - Detailing work history

  - Completing vocational testing

  - Assisting in collecting medical information essential to vocational planning

  - Making changes to increase employability

  - Contacting employers, schools, employment agencies, or other sources of information about selected vocations

  - Identifying academic requirements for a desired program or degree

- Counsel a client about resumes, interviewing, labor market trends, training resources, and dealing with fears about reentry into the workplace

- Identify a disability and evaluate its impact on vocational planning

- Discuss ways to structure support arrangements to create incentives and increased motivation to complete a vocational plan

- Testify as an expert about the earning capacity of the evaluated spouse

- Assist attorneys in developing interrogatories or cross-examination of opposing vocational experts for trials or mediation

- Reevaluate client to determine if there has been a good faith effort to comply with the job search or occupational plan from a prior vocational evaluation

- Evaluate the adequacy and appropriateness of job search efforts

DECIDING TO USE A VOCATIONAL EVALUATION

IF WORK AND EARNINGS ARE THE BASIS FOR ARGUMENTS ABOUT SUPPORT IN A DIVORCE, USE A VOCATIONAL EVALUATION

When one or more of the situations described below exists while a support amount is in dispute during a marital dissolution, accurate information on earning capacity from a vocational evaluation will help.

The analysis of a party's potential earnings and employability looks at both the person and the work world, and at the interaction between them. Influences from both sides, therefore, will have an impact on the outcomes of the evaluation and career planning. From the evaluee's side, personal or psychological dynamics come into play; from the world of work, general economic conditions, and detailed occupational factors enter the picture.

The kinds of concerns divorcing people have about work, familiar to family law attorneys, fall into identifiable categories. Parties' statements that exemplify these concerns are detailed in Chapter 6, so that attorneys can connect the problems expressed by their clients to the advisability of a vocational evaluation.

QUESTIONS ABOUT INDIVIDUAL CONCERNS THAT PROMPT A VOCATIONAL EVALUATION

Some possible *individual questions* or *interpersonal reasons* for a vocational evaluation during divorce support decisions are:

Reentry Problems

Reentry problems arise from the lack of any employment background or recent work experience and the natural fears prompted by thinking about going back to work. This is especially true if the reentry worker's prior work experience was not pleasant or fulfilling. The emotional and financial connections to spousal support also compound reentry fears.

Disability Issues

The evaluee's own medical or psychological problems can also activate an exploration of the possibility of disability. A supporting spouse may question the validity and work impact of the evaluee's health concerns. The evaluee may have anxieties about whether a physical or psychological condition will have a negative effect on the ability to work.

Disability issues can also emerge when a dependent child's welfare requires the evaluee's care to a degree that would interfere with that spouse's ability to work full or part time. This topic is more fully discussed in Chapter 6.

Motivation Questions

California courts assume motivation and willingness to work, but the behavior of divorcing parties may not always demonstrate these qualities. When spouses are not working full time or their incomes fall significantly, it is common to doubt their motivation to provide support or be self-supporting. When a spouse's income is not as large as expected, the other side often suspects that support obligations are the main driving factor. The supported spouse suspects that supporting spouse is suppressing income to lower his monthly checks; the supporting spouse suspects that the supported spouse is not giving a good faith effort to earn, to be awarded more support.

The vocational evaluation examines and describes behavior – actions and statements – and does not seek to analyze the underlying motivational state. Instead, the focus is on manifestations of cooperation or noncooperation and external indicators of motivation to work or not, that show up during vocational evaluations and reports. More on this topic is in Chapter 9.

Career Concerns

For active job seekers who are not finding work, the vocational counseling and coaching skills of the evaluator can help assess why the job seeker is not successfully connecting to the work world.

People who are not working, and even those who are, do not always make career choices based on sufficient information. These parties can bring to the vocational evaluation dreams of self-employment, career thoughts that are unlikely to result in employment, or of jobs that are unrealistic for individual reasons or because of labor market conditions. The evaluation is a place to bring a reality check to career ideas. Self-employment is explored in Chapter 5; the discussion of job search is also in Chapter 5.

QUESTIONS ABOUT THE LABOR MARKET THAT ACTIVATE A VOCATIONAL EVALUATION

In the analysis of the interaction between the evaluee and the world of work, labor market questions also trigger vocational evaluations. The labor market affects job choice, opportunities, and wages, and thus the outcomes of a vocational evaluation. If concerns arise about the impact of work and labor market aspects such as those below, a vocational evaluation can help answer them.

- the unemployment rate, generally or for a specific job title

- employer requirements for skills, education, and work experience for a particular job title

- the emergence of a new occupation or the phasing out of an old one

- the common demands of an occupation for travel or extended hours

- labor market competition in an occupation nationally or locally

- the existence of demand for an occupation within a reasonable commute distance

- compensation for a defined occupation or skill set, with varying levels of experience

The vocational evaluation is especially useful in documenting the data for the labor market based on statistical surveys, targeted employer information, and separate interviews with knowledgeable insiders, rather than on generic information or anecdotal impressions. More discussion of labor market research is in Chapter 8.

VOCATIONAL EVALUATIONS CAN HELP RELATIONSHIPS BETWEEN DIVORCING SPOUSES

Divorce is fraught with conflict that often does not end with the decision to separate. The conflicts leak into the legal wrangling to complete the decoupling of the spouses' lives and into the relationships with the lawyers, the children, and anyone else involved in the case. Depending on personalities, money, psychological strengths and weaknesses, and social standing, the parties often do not have, or feel they have, equal personal power to create the lives they want.

Perhaps one of the most disconcerting aspects of divorce for both spouses is the realization that they cannot influence each other the way they used to do. In the linkage of marriage, when one spouse acts, the other is affected. One spouse wants an advanced degree; the other works to support that wish. They want children so one parent works and the other spends much more time with the children and does not produce an income. Marital decisions made with mutual affection and shared values meant that the married couple both lived with the activity demands and financial consequences of each other's decisions.

We moved every two years, every time he got a promotion. So I would get the old house sold, the new house painted, the kids settled in schools, and then we'd do it all over again. We moved ten times in 19 years; of course, I didn't work. Now he wants me to earn a lot of money but I haven't worked since he started with this company.

With the bond between them broken by divorce, one spouse's decisions have less or no influence on the other's life except where family law intervenes or until each partner breaks the habit of accepting the other's influence. This change is hard for some spouses to accept, especially when it comes to financial matters.

Example A) The husband who is used to having a say over how to spend the money he earns can be infuriated by the existence of laws that define his financial obligation to the spouse he no longer values.

It's my money; I earn it. I work hard for it and if she wants money, she can go out and earn her own. She's smart. I'll give her some time till she's up and running, but this can't be a long term thing.

Example B) The wife can feel that promises made in the beginning of the relationship still hold even though the emotional bond that prompted them is broken.

We agreed that I would stay home with the children until they went off to college and that was the responsible way to raise children. We did not have kids to let someone else raise them. I know they're not babies now but they still need me and teens can get into worse trouble if a parent isn't around. I should get support until the kids are on their own. That's what he promised me.

Example C) One of the spouses, often the wife, still feels that the couple's power relationships still hold, although the spouses are no longer living together and the marital breach is irrevocable. The power that her wage-earning husband had over her choices still is part of her emotional makeup, even while she knows rationally that the marriage is over. This is more often true when the wife is unsure about how the court will hear her wishes and needs. She may be afraid that her powerful ex will have as much influence on the court's decisions as he did over her in the marriage. This habit of thinking can continue in her career planning.

I know what I want to do but my ex won't like it. He'll tell the court what he thinks I can do and they'll just order me to do what he thinks I should do. He wants me to go back to the job I had before we were married. I was good at it but I never liked it and I don't want to do it anymore. I just got into it because that's what I was supposed to do back then, but it was never my choice.

Example D) The supporting spouse has strong opinions about what job the supported spouse could and should do, and what salary that job should create. He wants his opinion to be influential in his ex-wife's career choice so that his support obligation is as low as possible.

What this spouse may find disconcerting is that his preference for his ex-wife's career no longer has a significant impact on her job options, as long as her career choice is a reasonable one. Her relationship with work is between her and the work world. Whether she would really be welcomed back, paid well, or hired at her previous job are all matters determined by the employers in the open labor market, not by his hopes.

Example E) The supported spouse has family obligations that can have an impact on her ability to work and create income. She may not realize that her ex-husband no longer has the emotional connection or the legal obligation to continue to take financial responsibility for this situation now that the couple is divorcing.

I can't work full time because my mother who is 88 is not doing well and I have to do her shopping and sometimes her cooking. I take her to the doctors more than three or four times a month and I have to stop in every day to make sure she's taking her pills. I can't add a full time job to that.

While married, spouses are accustomed to swaying each other's choices and use of the family income by their personal needs and desires. Personal choices such as a desire to attend school, pursue a creative career, work fewer hours, travel frequently, or spend unpaid time caring for family members will probably result in less income. The married couple accepts this financial result through shared aspirations and values.

In divorce, the couple no longer shares financial aspirations. The decision to create less income either has to be factored into the support equation or else clearly identified as one party's choice but not the other's shared responsibility. If a person who has spent time at home with the children requires further schooling to become employable, the trier of fact[3] (the family law court's judge or commissioner) may decide that the financial burden of a period of no income during school attendance is a joint responsibility. If, however, a person feels obliged to care for a disabled elder unrelated to the other spouse, the supporting spouse may not have to give extra financial support to compensate for the unpaid time spent on elder care.

The intervention of a legal system into a couple's mutually agreed decisions can be jarring. It feels foreign to many people with little familiarity with the law to have an outside person, a judge or mediator, mandating important parts of their personal lives. It takes time, and often a third party's information or advice, to help the naturally self-interested parties see how the law views divorce.

More discussion on this topic is in Chapter 2.

VOCATIONAL EVALUATIONS CAN HELP COMMUNICATION BETWEEN CLIENT AND ATTORNEY

Divorce is one of the major life traumas no matter how carefully it is handled, and the couple involved may undergo some of the worst times in their lives. Their pain is real and justified, their experiences new, raw, and deserving of an empathetic response. They require and expect help, and often do not differentiate between the advocacy roles of their attorneys and therapists and the still caring but neutral stance of the vocational evaluator.

Attorneys may work with their clients for months or even years. Over time, they can feel invested both professionally and emotionally in finishing the case to serve the best interests and expectations of that client. Attorneys gain added personal satisfaction from protecting their clients and receiving gratitude for their personal concern as well as their professional competence. Family law attorneys naturally want to earn their client's confidence that they can help in managing the court system and the trauma of the divorce. The downside of this closeness is that attorneys may be reluctant to announce negative outcomes to their clients, and clients may hold the attorneys personally responsible when things do not go their way.

By remaining objective, the vocational evaluator can function as a neutral expert voice outside the client-attorney relationship. This allows the attorney to inform the client about the expert's conclusions that may alert them to potential challenges to work and earnings, so that the client does not attribute the responsibility for the bad news to the attorney. Such messages can cause a breach in the close advocate rapport. As a third party separate from the attorney-client relationship, the neutral vocational expert can convey the significance of less than ideal news about potential support.

That being said, vocational evaluators often start their careers as counselors and do not lose the empathic awareness and impulse to help as they use their expertise to advise evaluees and attorneys.

The evaluator needs to balance between being emotionally attuned as a listener and being drawn into the drama of the parties' relationship, between assisting in drawing up a return to work method and trying to fix the pain by altering the vocational plan or expert opinions.

The expert often functions as a consultant to the attorney, sounding an alert to a potential flaw in the legal strategy.

IF WORK AND EARNINGS ARE KNOWN AND UNCONTESTED, NO VOCATIONAL EVALUATION IS NECESSARY

Vocational evaluations are very useful in those divorces when only one spouse is employed, or, in the case where they are both working, the earnings of one spouse are in dispute.

In some divorces, income from work is not a point of contention. He is working, she is not – or vice versa – and they both understand why. The next step – she is going to go to work – is clear to both of them and they agree on the likely results of this job plan.

I'm going back into nursing. My license is up to date and I've kept up with the field. I've taken all my refresher courses. I can call the recruiter at my old job and if they can't take me back, I have a couple other places in mind. I know what I'll earn; it's the standard union rate for nurses here.

In this situation, the wife's future earnings are foreseeable, her career idea is set and agreeable to both, and she knows how to find work and is reasonably sure she will be able to land a job. No vocational questions exist and a vocational evaluation is not necessary.

Another situation in which a vocational evaluation may not be valuable is if the likely findings will not change the support figures.

I'm retired from my state job and it's clear what my ex-wife will get as a share of my retirement. She hasn't worked in 15 years and her health isn't great, so I don't really expect her to earn a lot. Our calculations show that if she can only earn a small amount, my support payments won't go down much. She probably can't earn enough to make a real difference anyway.

WHAT A VOCATIONAL EVALUATION IS NOT

A vocational evaluation is a defined process based on professional methodology employed by experts to reach conclusions. It is not a weapon or a legal or emotional threat.

- It is not a way to retaliate or take revenge against the evaluee or the evaluee's ex-spouse.

- It is not a way for the referring spouse to continue by proxy to abuse and control the evaluated spouse.

- It is not a way to make the spouse keep promises made in the marriage, implicit or explicit, that family law does not support.

- It is not a way for an evaluated or referring spouse to hire the vocational evaluator as another advocate.

One family law attorney's web site states, "A vocational evaluation is a tool…it is a way to intimidate a non-working spouse."

A vocational evaluation may be part of an attorney's strategy to settle the case, but it is NOT a means to intimidate. It is hard enough for both parties to go through the divorce; the vocational evaluation process should not be further punishment.

> A vocational evaluation should feel to the evaluee as an opportunity to be heard, to have his or her interests taken seriously, and to be treated respectfully.
>
> A vocational evaluation is an interactive, two-way process with unbiased information and feedback to enable the evaluee to make informed career decisions.

THE LEGAL BASIS FOR VOCATIONAL EVALUATIONS IN FAMILY LAW

California courts have said "We recognize that it is in the best interests of both spouses and of society in general that the supported spouse become self-sufficient" and that "the goal [is] that the supported party shall be self-supporting within a reasonable period of time." (CA Family Law Code 4331 – See Appendix C)

The vocational evaluation describes the particulars of what reasonable means when discussing the supported spouse's "reasonable efforts to assist in providing for his or her support needs" and in "reasonable period of time," and specifies what appropriate means in "appropriate period of time to be self-supporting."

FAMILY LAW CODE – PURPOSE OF VOCATIONAL EVALUATION

California Family Law Code (See Appendices B, C, D) describes the fundamental purpose of the vocational examination (also known as an evaluation or assessment) of earning capacity. The vocational examination is an expert's assessment of a spouse's ability to obtain employment that would allow the party to maintain herself or himself as close as possible to the marital standard of living.

FAMILY LAW CODE – ELEMENTS TO BE CONSIDERED

The life circumstances that must be considered under the law to establish employability are the evaluee's age, health, education, marketable skills, and the labor market demand for those skills. These are commonly seen in the laws of many states (Tracy & Wallace, 2008). The California Family Code also calls for the details of any education the evaluee needs to acquire additional marketable skills.

FAMILY LAW CODE AND CASE LAW – EXPECTATION OF SELF-SUPPORT

The California Family Code establishes the expectation that both parties will contribute to their own self-support to the best of their abilities. The analysis of those abilities is a focus of the vocational evaluation.

The interpretation of the Family Code derives from case law decisions that rise to the level of judicial notice. These decisions become precedent on which future legal decisions depend.

In a move away from the prior expectation that in some marriages (usually those of longer than ten years' duration), spousal support will continue for the spouse's life, the California Supreme Court shifted its policy to reflect the changes in opportunities for women in the labor force. The Court modified spousal support from permanent support to "one that entitles either spouse to post dissolution support for only so long as is necessary to become self-supporting." (Schmir, CA 2005) By the late 1970s, the percentage of women who work while parenting children under the age of 17 was starting to rise (BLS, 2010) from less than half to more than 70 percent in 2009. The Morrison (CA 1978) court, in recognition of women's increasing ability to earn, helped to establish the need for vocational evaluations by stating that the court needed "evidence in the record" about "a supported spouse's ability to meet his or her future needs" to rely on for decisions about support. The court "must not engage in speculation" when considering terminating support in lengthy marriages. The Morrison court also stated that, "It certainly may be inferred that … the Legislature intended that all supported spouses who were able to do so should seek employment." This established the need to assess ability to work.

CASE LAW SUMMARY

Morrison (CA 1978)

Morrison stated explicitly that all supported spouses who were able to work should seek employment, and that the court needed evidence, not speculation, about "a spouse's ability to meet his or her future needs" to set accurate support levels.

This finding established the basis for vocational evaluations to provide evidence and that assessing ability to work should be part of the vocational evaluation.

Several cases clarified the method by which the spouse is informed of the court's expectation that she or he would contribute to self-support.

The Richmond (CA 1980) case found that a spouse must be informed of the need to make efforts toward self-support. The rulings in this case establish the use of a court order that lays out the expectation of self-support: "The effect of a 'Richmond' order is to tell each spouse that the supported spouse has a specified period of time to become self-supporting, after which the obligation of the supporting spouse will cease."

CASE LAW SUMMARY

Richmond (CA 1980)

A *Richmond* order tells each spouse that the supported spouse has a specified period of time to become self-supporting, after which the spousal support obligation will end. It also set the requirement that evidence, not speculation, of earning capacity is necessary.

For a Richmond order to be effective and fair, the court must make the spouse aware that the law expects that he or she will attempt to become self-supporting. The rationale for notifying the spouse about time limits of support with a Richmond order is contained in Gavron (CA 1988). The Gavron court held that a supported spouse must "have some reasonable advance warning that after an appropriate period of time the supported spouse was expected to become self-sufficient or face onerous legal and financial consequences."

CASE LAW SUMMARY
Gavron (CA 1988)
Per *Gavron*, the court must warn a spouse that she or he is expected to become self-supporting by a specified date. If the warning has been given, the court can terminate support at that date.

A Gavron warning was mandatory at first but is now discretionary, as seen in the use of the word "may" in the Family Code Section 4320 as:

When making an order for spousal support, the court may advise the recipient of support that he or she should make reasonable efforts to assist in providing for his or her support needs, taking into account the particular circumstances considered by the court pursuant to [Family Code] section 4320, unless, in the case of a marriage of long duration as provided for in [Family Code] section 4336, the court decides this warning is inadvisable.

Even if a formal Gavron warning is not issued, as in the Schmir case (CA 2005), the court found that the order for a vocational evaluation served as notice to the spouse that she was expected to become self-supporting. The Schmir court stated that, "Spouses who need further education or training to become employable will usually need more advance warning than spouses who already possess job skills and only need to find suitable work. It is not possible to set a minimum or maximum warning time."

CASE LAW – EARNING CAPACITY DEFINED

The California Civil Practice Guide on Family Law (Hogoboom & King, 2008-2011) citing the Everett (CA 1990) and Simpson (CA1992) cases, states that

"Earning capacity" is not defined in the statutes. However, statutory references to the measure of a spouse's ability to obtain employment as well as decisions defining earning capacity in various contexts suggest that for purposes of determining support, "earning capacity" represents the income that a spouse is reasonably capable of earning based upon the spouse's age, health, education, marketable skills, employment history, and the availability of employment opportunities.

Courts require evidence, not speculation, of earning capacity on which to base support determinations. This judicial opinion is also seen in Richmond (CA 1980) which says that it is reasonable for the court to set a limitation or termination date on spousal support after a lengthy marriage, but the timing "may not be arbitrary or based upon speculation as to the supported spouse's future employment qualifications or opportunities." Instead, the trial court requires clear evidence in the record that the supported spouse will be able to meet his or her financial needs adequately at the time selected for termination of jurisdiction.

A vocational evaluation or examination with a vocational plan to become self-supporting can furnish that evidence.

Tracy and Wallace (2010), in summarizing the family law cases nationally defining earning capacity found that:

Only a few states define earning capacity through case law, those being California, Florida, and Louisiana. In the marriage of Regnery (CA 1989) earning capacity was defined as being composed of (1) the ability to work, taking into account such factors as age, occupation, skills, education, health, background, work experience and qualifications; (2) the willingness to work as exemplified through good faith efforts, due diligence and meaningful attempts to secure employment; and (3) the opportunity to work as evidenced by the availability of job openings.

Later the California courts, recognizing that the second element of willingness to work should be taken for granted, recast Regnery's three-prong test as a simple two-prong test: ability and opportunity." So long as a parent has an earning capacity, that is, the ability and the opportunity to earn income, the trial court may attribute income. (Destein [CA 2001])

Tracy and Wallace noted further that the Bardzik case clarified that the definition of earning capacity includes both ability to work and opportunity to work, but excludes the question of whether the individual would in fact be hired. These elements as outlined in Regnery and further clarified in Bardzik — the factors of ability and opportunity — set a foundation for determining an individual's employability and earning capacity by vocational experts.

CASE LAW SUMMARY

Regnery (CA 1989)

Regnery formulated the "need to show ability and opportunity to work to establish earning capacity".

CASE LAW – EVIDENCE OF ABILITY AND OPPORTUNITY TO WORK

The Bardzik (CA 2008) case established a strong basis for using a vocational expert with this finding.

If one parent seeks to *modify* an existing order so as to have income imputed to the other parent, the parent seeking imputation…bears the burden of proof of showing that the other parent has the ability and opportunity to earn that imputed income.

CASE LAW SUMMARY
Bardzik (CA 2008)

Bardzik established that if a parent wants to change child support, that parent has the burden of proof to present competent evidence that the other parent has an earning capacity.

The proof of earning capacity must be competent evidence presented to the court, not just an unsupported statement. This mandate was made in the case of Wittgrove (CA 2004) where a parent who wanted to impute income based on the other parent's presumed earning capacity failed to present any competent evidence that the other parent had the ability or opportunity to earn that income.

The case of Smith (CA 2001) also established a requirement for evidence in its definition of opportunity to work. The "opportunity to work" exists when there is substantial evidence of a reasonable "likelihood that a party could, with reasonable effort, apply his or her education, skills and training to produce income." The finding in Cohn (CA 1998) about how the earning capacity is calculated states: "[F]igures for earning capacity cannot be drawn from thin air; they must have some tangible evidentiary foundation."

CASE LAW SUMMARY
Wittgrove (CA 2004)
Smith (CA 2001)
Cohn (CA 1998)

Wittgrove set the precedent that competent evidence is necessary to meet the burden of proof that ability and opportunity to earn income exist.

Smith called for substantial evidence of the likelihood that a party could produce income.

The appellate court in *Cohn* mandated solid evidence to impute income: "[F]igures for earning capacity cannot be drawn from thin air; they must have some tangible evidentiary foundation."

Vocational evaluations fill in the blank spaces in family law cases, where basic questions like "What can you earn and when?" and "What are you going to do for work?" need answers. Adding expert advice to the divorce, when the parties do not know the answers, averts decisions not based on factual evidence.

◆◆◆

A vocational examination is the method to present competent and substantial evidence, a tangible evidentiary foundation to meet the burden of proof about opportunity to work and earning capacity.

CHAPTER TWO – THE VOCATIONAL EVALUATOR

Where talents and the needs of the world cross, therein lies your vocation.

Aristotle (384-322 BC)

THE KNOWLEDGE AND SKILLS OF A VOCATIONAL EVALUATOR

Using the expertise of vocational counselors and vocational rehabilitation counselors in forensic settings is a relatively new application of these skills. *Forensic* refers to the use of vocational evaluations or assessments in a legal setting. Any legal case that concerns the issues of ability to work, capacity to earn, and opportunity to find employment can use vocational evaluations. Currently, vocational counselors help in forensic cases regarding the determination of eligibility for Social Security Disability benefits, workers' compensation and long-term disability benefits, employment law and personal injury damages, as well as in family law.

Forensic vocational assessment is an expansion of the professional tasks of rehabilitation counselors, although "it is not often promoted as a viable means of employment" for counselors. (Donnell et al., 2004) The essential knowledge base of a vocational evaluator in family law derives not only from the mandates of state law, but from the skills and best practices in vocational counseling and vocational rehabilitation counseling. "Over time, the role, function and scope of practice of rehabilitation counselors have evolved into a well-established profession with established methods, protocols and standards of practice." (Robinson, 2011)

These sources offer guidance for vocational evaluators and those who work with these experts.

Of the ten[4] core areas of knowledge and skills essential for effective rehabilitation counseling practice (Leahy et al., 1993), five are most applicable in family law vocational evaluation practice, which does not emphasize the rehabilitation aspect of the profession. To these, Deutsch and Sawyer (1990) add experience with clients. This experience "enriches learned knowledge domains and increases understanding of issues impacting workability." Sleister (2000) notes the vocational expert should have further knowledge domains and skills.

Leahy et al. (1998) listed the important areas of knowledge for counselors who practice in private sector rehabilitation rather than for government rehabilitation agencies. Vocational experts in private practice mostly assess and testify about work prospects for people with disabilities, as in workers' compensation and Social Security cases, but many also work in family law. Some items within their knowledge domains apply less to the field of family law evaluations (such as psychosocial and functional aspects of disability, job analysis and accommodations).

The following list contains the knowledge domains that are most applicable to the performance of family law evaluations. These collated fields of professional knowledge and skills describe what an expert vocational evaluator knows and can do:

- vocational counseling, evaluation and consultation services

- individual and group counseling

- family, gender, and multicultural issues

- environmental and attitudinal barriers to work

- vocational assessment

- vocational planning

- available community resources

- experience working with clients

- transferability of skills and worker traits

- evaluation of personal characteristics and past work history

- current labor market trends and conditions

- articulation of findings of vocational status in both written and oral formats

- case management and reporting

- expert testimony

- legislation and regulations

- family law and case findings applicable to family law

FAMILY LAW CODE – QUALIFICATIONS OF A VOCATIONAL EVALUATOR

Although the California Family Code Section 4331(d) designates the evaluator as the "vocational training counselor" to conduct the vocational examination, this terminology does not correspond with any structured university degree program or professional certification. The vocational counseling field does not use the term vocational training counselor and there is no such major at any college or graduate school, or any professional organization of vocational training counselors.

The Code thus does not narrowly define the exact professional background of people who can conduct a vocational evaluation. The section describes the qualifications of the Master's level professional as a person educated in the behavioral sciences with knowledge, skill, experience, training, and education in interviewing, administering, and interpreting tests for analysis of marketable skills, formulating career ideas, planning courses of training and study, and assessing the job market. This list of skills and knowledge makes clear the legislative intent that a vocational plan may be one of the major anticipated outcomes of the vocational evaluation when the evaluee needs this service.

THE ROLE OF THE VOCATIONAL EVALUATOR

Under the ethics codes of some professional organizations, the combined assignments — to determine earning capacity evaluation and to deliver client services around vocational questions — could be considered a dual role for a vocational evaluator, that is, functioning both as evaluating expert and as advising counselor.

In California family law, however, vocational evaluators conduct the vocational evaluation and career planning simultaneously in an integrated methodology under a legal mandate to do both. If family law did not call for both as part of family law vocational evaluations, these two services might be accomplished sequentially by a single evaluator, or by two different professionals. Since earning capacity is specific to a job title, however, the two are inextricably linked.

This explicit message from the Family Code, that the evaluator is to help both the court and/or attorneys with earnings projections and the evaluee with career planning, makes it important that the evaluator understand this duality and avoid forging alliances that would compromise one of the outcomes to benefit the other. It also is important that the evaluator explain this relationship to the evaluee clearly. The potential for bias lies in compromising the career choice recommendations to fulfill the desires of the requesting party, or slanting the evaluation conclusions to conform to the preferences of the evaluee without consideration of their impact on the opposing side.

These aspects of the vocational evaluation are a necessary part of the initial discussion with the evaluee, so that participation can progress with the evaluee's informed consent. Even when the court has ordered the evaluee to participate in the evaluation, informed consent is essential. The disclosure discussion is the necessary step to inform the evaluee about the evaluator's role. Evaluator bias is a frequent evaluee concern. Addressing it immediately helps to reduce this worry and to ensure a fair and ethical exchange of information.

PROFESSIONAL CODES OF ETHICS

Several professional organizations address the requirement to inform the evaluee about the evaluation process in their codes of ethics.

Not all evaluators belong to one of the major professional organizations that publish Codes of Ethics, such as those below, because evaluators come from many different educational and experiential backgrounds. However, the Codes give broadly applicable guidance for ethical behavior for vocational evaluators with varying qualifications.

One common professional background for a vocational expert comes from training as a vocational rehabilitation counselor. A major national standard for professional achievement as a vocational rehabilitation counselor is the Certified Rehabilitation Counselor (CRC) designation. Vocational counselors with CRCs work nationally in a wide variety of settings and under many different kinds of legal and regulatory mandates. Some work in state rehabilitation agencies, private practices, or nonprofit services; others serve clients in nonforensic situations, such as those receiving Workers' Compensation or disability insurance payments; other vocational counselors practice in forensic situations such as family law, personal injury, or litigated insurance cases. These varied practices have many sources of funding (state/federal, nonprofit, insurance policies, or employment benefits) as well as private funding in family law.

The CRC Code of Ethics (Commission on Rehabilitation Counselor Certification, 2011) anticipates that its professional members offer different services in a sequence of relationships that can change over time. The CRC Code of Ethics for Rehabilitation Counselors[5] states:

Section A 5(f): ROLE CHANGES IN THE PROFESSIONAL RELATIONSHIP. When rehabilitation counselors change roles from the original or most recent contracted relationship, they obtain informed consent from clients or evaluees and explain the right to refuse services related to the change. Examples of role changes include: (1) changing from individual to group, relationship or family counseling, or vice versa; (2) changing from a forensic to a primary care role, or vice versa; (3) changing from a nonforensic evaluative role to a rehabilitation or therapeutic role, or vice versa; (4) changing from a rehabilitation counselor to a researcher role (e.g., enlisting clients as research participants), or vice versa; and, (5) changing from a rehabilitation counselor to a mediator role, or vice versa. The clients or evaluees must be fully informed of any anticipated consequences (e.g., financial, legal, personal, or therapeutic) due to a role change by the rehabilitation counselor.

The American Board of Vocational Experts (ABVE) is a national professional credentialing not-for-profit organization representing vocational experts in both the private and the public sectors. ABVE was founded in 1980 to preserve the integrity, standards, ethics, and uniqueness of vocational experts. (American Board of Vocational Experts, 2011)

The ABVE Code of Ethics (2007) states in its Rules of Professional Conduct:

R2.4 When Vocational Experts provide services at the request of a third party, the Vocational Expert clarifies the nature of the relationship to all involved parties. As a case consultant or expert witness, the Vocational Expert has an obligation to provide unbiased, fair and reasonable opinions.

R6.5 When an evaluee has been referred by a plaintiff or defense attorney, legal representative of the evaluee, government body or organization, a Vocational Expert can rely upon the Doctrine of Implied Consent, which means that the evaluee has given their consent for the evaluation. However, even under this rule, a discussion with the evaluee as to the purpose of the evaluation and how the evaluation results will be used should be discussed with the evaluee.

The International Association of Rehabilitation Professionals (IARP) includes 2,500 rehabilitation professionals practicing in the fields of long-term disability and disability management consulting, case management and managed care, forensics and expert testimony, life care planning, and Americans with Disabilities Act (ADA) consulting.

The IARP Code of Ethics, Standards of Practice and Competencies (International Association of Rehabilitation Professionals, 2007) states:

A2) At the outset and throughout the professional relationship, members will disclose to their clients professional boundaries, particularly if those involve multiple services on the same case where there exists a high potential for ethical conflict.

THE DISCLOSURE DISCUSSION

The vocational evaluator's role can be confusing to the evaluee. The evaluator should clarify at the outset what the normal outcomes of the evaluation are and how the evaluator and evaluee achieve them.

Often the evaluator's first question is, *"Do you know why you're here?"* It is rare to hear anything that indicates much understanding of what the evaluation is about, but the answers often sound like these:

My spouse's attorney said I had to come to you. I don't know what it's about but it's probably going to end up with me getting less money. That's what I'm afraid of, anyway.

You're supposed to tell me what I can do and then the court's going to make me do it whether I want to or not. Just another horrible part of this horrible divorce, I guess.

It is the vocational evaluator's responsibility to inform the evaluee early in the contact sequence about the nature of the evaluation and the role of the evaluator. In the initial meeting or while setting it up, the evaluator clarifies these most important points: non-confidentiality and neutrality.

NONCONFIDENTIALITY

The information gathered in the vocational evaluation is not confidential. The strategic purpose of the evaluation is to develop information to share with the entire legal team and the court so that the decisions about the dissolution are based on expert opinion.

Stating this clearly gives evaluees the understanding that they are in control of what they decide to say, and what they choose to reveal of their personal information.

Even though evaluations may be court ordered or initiated by the opposing spouse's attorney, it is common for someone to become so comfortable while speaking to a vocational expert — a good listener with a real interest in the person's background and feeling — that she or he wants to reveal important information. Career planning touches many personal aspects of a person's life – personality, values, culture, money, health, relationships, independence, parenting, and the vision of her or his place in the world. When done well, the evaluee wants to share information, and the evaluator wants to know who the person is so that the career fits the person well.

Many evaluees say, *"I've never told my ex about this, but ..."* Personal revelations that are relevant to vocational planning are especially important, and the evaluator cannot promise to keep them secret.

Even after a discussion about the fact that information shared in vocational evaluations is not confidential, some evaluees reveal personal details like these, and then ask *"Can we keep this secret?"*

> *I can't read. I was never diagnosed as dyslexic but I think I am, and I can't really read a newspaper. Only my mother knows, I've never told my husband. He calls me stupid. Does he have to know?*

The answer: yes, the dyslexia has to be disclosed. Learning disabilities can be closely tied to job choices, earnings, and school planning. They have to be part of the report. However, there are many ways to approach this information.

> *I have a conviction and I spent time in jail. I stole some building materials from my employer and got arrested. I met my wife after it happened and I've never told her. But it means that I can't get certain kinds of jobs, doesn't it? And I can't use that employer as a reference.*

The answer: not necessarily; revealing the conviction can be optional. The evaluator may not need to disclose the conviction in the report if it will have no major employment impact. For instance, if the offense was a misdemeanor, or in a juvenile record, expunged, or took place long ago, it may not affect the current employment picture. If questioned by the court or an attorney, the evaluator may have to divulge this to explain any limitations on the vocational options available to the evaluee. Felony convictions and other legal actions related to the evaluee's profession or occupation may have a significant impact on future employment. Serious legal problems that influence future employment will definitely become part of the evaluation and report.

The evaluator will probably disclose negative legal histories in the vocational evaluation report if the facts are public. For example, a professional who loses a license to practice his or her profession is probably not able to keep this fact confidential. An executive whose company has been sued for a major offence may have been named in a newspaper article about the event. Since even expunged records are not sealed from public inspection and the court file is a public record, the evaluee may want to investigate what information is available if an employer does a background check. The evaluator can help by coaching the job seeker about job interview skills to practice discussing difficult work histories with potential employers.

I was married before, just for a short time after high school. Does that have to go into the report?

The answer: no, it is probably not necessary to mention this in the report because it is not germane to future employment.

I think I'm drinking too much, but I kept it together when my wife and I were together, so I don't think she knows. I can't get through the day without it. I don't know how I'll work, but I don't want her to know.

The answer: The wife probably knows more than he imagines she does. If alcohol or drug intake poses a barrier to employment, the evaluator would normally reveal it as a significant issue in a vocational evaluation report. However, not all alcohol use poses an employment problem.

The evaluee should understand that the vocational evaluation report may be filed with the court and become part of the public record, so any revelation has to be discussed with that in mind. The evaluator has the discretion to omit irrelevant but embarrassing information, but will probably disclose any information with an impact on vocational planning. For example, dyslexia may require extended time for schooling; treatment for alcoholism may require time and financial support. Disbarment or loss of a professional license may necessitate a change of occupation.

One method to keep confidential information out of the vocational report, even if it has a vocational implication, is with the informed agreement of both attorneys and both parties. If there is open communication between the attorneys, especially with a good reason to protect the public reputation of the couple, the background information can be unstated. This could be applicable if the parties are well-known or public figures. The vocational conclusions would not change, but the evaluator does not have to describe the underlying reasons for them if everyone agrees to this arrangement.

An alternative to this is if the parties request that the court seal the records involved in the divorce so that they are not searchable as public records. A basic principle is that the vocational evaluation should be managed so as not to harm the evaluee's future prospects for employment, if possible.

In the case of Carla, the woman who could not read, we spent some time exploring resources: testing for dyslexia, community college support for her as a student who probably has a disability, financial and other help she might receive from the Department of Rehabilitation, and even how to apply. We also rehearsed what she would say to her husband, children, and other family members.

Carla returned for her next appointment with a smile, reporting that she had told a few family members about her reading problem for the first time in her life. She felt as if a burden was lifting. Her lifelong shameful secret was transforming into a problem many people have, not a disgrace. She now could explain that she was not stupid, she just had a learning disorder. Carla realized that her son's learning difficulties were similar to hers and she was now willing to talk to his school about helping him. The information was not confidential and became part of the vocational report, but the revelation did not harm the evaluee.

NEUTRALITY

The evaluator is a neutral expert, no matter who has hired her or him, and no matter who has paid for the services.

A vocational evaluation should feel to evaluees as an opportunity to be heard, to have their interests taken seriously, and to be treated respectfully. It is an interactive, two-way process with unbiased information and feedback to enable the evaluee to make informed career decisions. This does not mean that the conclusions will necessarily conform to the evaluee's wishes, but if they do not, the evaluee will have had a chance to explain his or her perspective and will hear the reasoning for the evaluator's conclusions.

The vocational evaluation report is a fair and complete statement of facts with all the conclusions supported by evidence, research if needed, and data.

Evaluator neutrality makes these outcomes possible. Explaining that this is the stance and commitment of the evaluator reassures the evaluee and makes possible the informed consent to participate.

EVALUATING BOTH SPOUSES

In some divorces, both spouses question the other's income production. For a nonworking spouse, the questions from the opposing side will concern job choice and salaries, or whether the job search is adequate. For a working spouse, the questions will address whether the income is representative of a good faith effort to work and earn money. An evaluator can see both spouses as separate evaluees.

With attention paid to each as an independent individual, the evaluation describes each spouse's relationship to the world of work, not to each other's expectations. The evaluator is careful not to convey any private, non-work-related information from one spouse (e.g., affairs, abuse allegations, personality traits, financial dealings) in the conclusions about the spouse under evaluation. The evaluator incorporates in the report only the information from the spouse about that spouse, unless the opposing party has information directly applicable to the work life of the other.

The evaluator is also careful not to disclose to the second evaluee of the pair any private information learned in the first evaluation.

THE DISCLOSURE DOCUMENT

In addition to the discussion about the vocational evaluation steps, the evaluator gives the evaluee a written document with the same information.

A sample disclosure document is in Appendix F. Because the evaluee may distrust the evaluator hired by the opposing side, the evaluator does not ask the evaluee to sign the document, especially without consultation with and agreement of the evaluee's attorney. The evaluator fills in his or her own signature and date to confirm that the discussion has happened and gives a copy of the signed disclosure form to the evaluee. The signed original stays in the case file.

MAINTAINING NEUTRALITY

Maintaining the evaluator's neutral stance is both essential and difficult. Evaluators in their counseling function develop empathy for the situation of the evaluee; evaluators as paid professionals have an interest in continuing positive relationships with referral sources for their own financial self-interest.

Both of these forces press on the evaluator's judgment and inclinations. Other considerations may serve to equalize these pressures. For vocational evaluators in private practice, and most of

California's evaluators are, neutrality is not only the ethical way to function but a wise business strategy for long term practice survival.

Most experienced family law attorneys prefer to rely on the earnings projections of a neutral expert for realistic support planning. Fair vocational suggestions are more useful to the evaluee and more credible to the court. A Practice Pointer from the *California Practice Guide: Family Law* (Hogoboom & King, 2007) advises attorneys on how to choose a neutral vocational counselor for the vocational evaluation. *"Apart from the minimum statutory qualifications, the reputation of the proposed counselor in the local community is also important. It is a waste of time and money to choose a counselor who has a reputation for finding that virtually anyone can work regardless of age, health or lack of job skills; the court is likely to give his or her opinion little weight."*

The evaluator's job is not to confirm the divorcing spouse's opinions, or to make the attorney's support calculations higher or lower. The vocational evaluator does not make decisions about spousal and child support, but reports information as accurately as possible to the parties, their attorneys, and the triers of fact to make these decisions. Neutrality involves providing as much significant information as possible and explicitly identifying gaps in available information so that the trier of fact can evaluate the value of the information reported. Deliberate omission of inconvenient facts is not neutrality.

Some divorcing spouses who are *in pro per* — representing themselves without the aid of an attorney[6] — request evaluations. The spouse who is making the initial call, writing the check, and staying in contact with the vocational expert may not have any experience of hiring a neutral expert and could confuse the vocational expert's position with that of an advocate who is on his or her side.

The *in pro per* divorcing spouse, representing himself, might say,

> *I need a vocational evaluation to show that my ex can earn more income. I haven't seen any effort to find work and I'm tired of shelling out support money to let her sit at home and do nothing. So I'll expect you to write a report that shows how there are plenty of jobs out there that an educated person can do.*

This may or may not be a reasonable request based on the facts of the case, but the neutral vocational evaluator will make sure that the caller hears in the initial contact that an ethical professional cannot guarantee a precise outcome. The *in pro per* caller should know, before signing an agreement to proceed and paying for services, that the conclusions from the evaluation may or may not result in lowering support payments. This offers the caller enough information to make a decision about whether she or he wants to invest in the vocational evaluation at all.

Fees cover the expert's time to develop information and the expert advice and neutral conclusions that will stand up under scrutiny. The shape of the opinion is not for sale. Without this understanding, it may be a waste of the caller's time to proceed.

PRACTICAL STEPS EVALUATORS CAN TAKE TO SUPPORT THEIR NEUTRALITY

- If a referral source asks that the evaluator not consider a major element listed in the Family Code, such as age, health, or skills, the evaluator should make clear that the conclusions reached could change if information about these issues were incorporated into the assignment

Because the Family Code lists age and health, among others, as factors that affect employability, the evaluator must include these to form a set of conclusions that complies with the law. In accepting a truncated assignment, experts have to be concerned about their independence. If the attorney or other referral source defines a restricted scope of the evaluation, the evaluator makes it clear that the evaluation and thus its conclusions have limitations. Not making the limitations explicit can compromise the expert's professional neutrality.

- The evaluator accepts information from all sources but assesses its applicability, its source, its relevance, and its reliability before relying on it for the formation of any vocational conclusions.

- In the report, the evaluator lists all the information received and its sources and specifies what information she or he relied on to draw the report conclusions.

The opposing spouse may offer the evaluator information about the evaluee, especially if that spouse's attorney has proposed the evaluation. The spouse may feel that he has hired "his" expert as an extension of the attorney relationship and that the attorney's advocacy function extends to the vocational evaluation. It is important to be open to accept information from all sources with pertinent data, including a referring spouse, but equally important to use expert judgment to assess the applicability of that information to the vocational position of the evaluee.

Spouses often feel that they have to make sure that the charm or personality of the evaluee does not sway the evaluator. After the marriage relationship has shifted from love strong enough to inspire a wedding to conflict grim enough to split the couple apart, spouses sometimes feel that they were manipulated into falling for the wrong person. Ex-partners seem to worry that the evaluee's attractiveness will deceive the evaluator, much as they feel they were at the beginning of the marriage, or that the evaluator will be as influenced as they were by the spouse's power and persuasiveness during the marriage. Even though they are divorcing, some spouses still see their ex's personal magnetism as so strong, perhaps overwhelming, that they expect others to be overcome also. They fear the ex is so convincing and cogent that the evaluator will just follow her or his lead.

Alternatively, they worry that the ex-spouse will lie in the evaluation and try to look less skilled and intelligent, less employable, less capable than the partner thinks he or she is.

Evaluators do not have the same responses to the evaluee as ex-spouses do; they have seen many people in similar circumstances. The evaluation methodology includes a thorough vocational interview with other confirming information that elicits a full range of applicable vocational information. The complete process has depth and is not a superficial impression of an evaluee's personality. The evaluator compares information from many life events, so that education and work history, earnings histories and experience, activities of daily living and reasons for life changes all contribute to a full and accurate foundation for the evaluator's conclusions.

Referring spouses may want to supplement the evaluator's file with detailed information about the employability prospects of the evaluee. This is especially common if the two parties have been working in the same industry, such as high tech, or marketing, or financial services, where they both have expertise in the employment practices of the field. This information is valuable but the evaluator must validate it with independent fact gathering and research. Otherwise, the expert's report is merely a restatement of the spouse's opinions, not a neutral view of the evaluee's employment options and opportunities.

Because the vocational evaluator is assessing the relationship between the evaluee and the world of work, the acceptability of the evaluee as a potential employee is determined between that evaluee and employers, as researched and reported by the evaluator. Unless a party in the litigation case is planning to offer the evaluee a job, opinions of the parties and their attorneys about the evaluee's earning capacity present minimal or no guidance about the evaluee's employability, and have little relevance to the conclusions drawn in the evaluation. The employee-employer relationship is outside the scope of the litigation, the divorce, and the marriage; the independent report from the vocational expert should reflect that distance.

One conscientious husband called me to ask what he should do to help the evaluation. "What's my role in this?" he asked. "To read my report," I answered. He laughed.

- The evaluator does not promise particular answers or conclusions.

An expert who accepts an assignment with a predetermined outcome is no longer neutral and his or her conclusions are of little use to the trier of fact. The expert who agrees to accept a case to find a definite result but does not produce that outcome is making a deceptive commitment to the referral source. It is more honest to state explicitly that as a neutral, the expert cannot accept any case assignment with a promise to find a predetermined outcome, leaving the referral source free to accept or reject this approach to the evaluation.

In connection with not promising an exact outcome, a vocational expert should not accept payment arrangements contingent on the way the case is decided, or on whether the vocational information proves sufficient to influence the support decisions.

- The evaluator does not assume the role of the evaluee's champion.

◆ ◆ ◆

The skilled vocational expert with the background mandated by the state's law and with the education and experience of a professional vocational counselor follows the codes of ethics of the professional organizations to which she or he belongs. Maintaining neutrality is the strongest expression of professionalism. Informed participation of the evaluee is essential.

CHAPTER THREE – STARTING THE VOCATIONAL EVALUATION

Your work is to discover your work and then with all your heart to give yourself to it.

Buddha

IDENTIFYING THE NEED FOR A VOCATIONAL EVALUATION

The initiator of a vocational evaluation is most often a family law attorney, mediator, or judge or commissioner in a Superior Court. The attorney or judge has a question about the earning capacity of one of the divorcing spouses and wants expert information to make a recommendation or settlement offer regarding reasonable spousal support, child support, or family support. The examination can also be initiated by a divorcing spouse, either representing himself or herself (*in pro per*) or represented.

CASE SITUATIONS THAT PROBABLY NEED A VOCATIONAL EVALUATION

Since most people outside of family law do not know about vocational evaluations, it is unusual for a divorcing client to ask for the service by name. They and their lawyers may not recognize the signals that a vocational evaluation will be helpful. However, circumstances such as those below will be a good indicator of the necessity of initiating a vocational evaluation.

The majority of cases involve the evaluation of a nonworking spouse, usually the wife, of a working spouse, usually the husband. Vocational evaluations are effective in many other divorce situations: working wife/nonworking husband; both spouses working; both spouses not working.

Family Law Case Situations That Need a Vocational Evaluation	
Reentry Problems	**Can Sound Like This**
A spouse is not working.	*I'm raising three children and I have to be at home after school. That's when kids need supervision and parenting and it's very important that I be there. The time when they're in school, I spend cleaning and shopping and cooking. And there has to be some time for me in there somewhere.*
A court has issued a Seek-Work Order but the spouse is not working after an extended time has passed.	*I know I had the Seek Work Order three years ago but I had to sell the house and move, and get the kids set up, and I've tried, but I haven't found jobs.*
A spouse states that s/he is not employable but both parties do not agree upon the reason.	*A: I can't work because no one will hire me and there are no jobs I can do. Employers don't hire people my age.* *B: That's not true. You were offered a job just last month*
A spouse is unsure of a vocational goal.	*I have no idea what I can do. I only worked at a few jobs before we got married.*
A spouse has no recent work experience.	*I haven't done anything but volunteer work since my first child was born, and she's almost 17 now.*
A spouse expresses fear of going to work.	*Even the idea of looking for work makes me start shaking. I get so scared. I've never been really good at talking to people and I have no idea about how to do this.*

Family Law Case Situations That Need a Vocational Evaluation	
Disability Concerns	**Can Sound Like This**
A spouse has or claims a disability that may affect vocational choice or success.	*I have a medical condition that flares about every three weeks or so and then I'm down for several days. Sometimes I can't leave the house and I have to have the carpool take the kids to school. I try to push through it but I don't see how I can really work.*
A dependent child requires care that may have an impact on a custodial parent's ability to work	*My son has been diagnosed with a bunch of problems and he has had an IEP since kindergarten. I have to get him to the therapist, the speech therapist, his tutors, and he has a special diet, too. I have to work with him every night on schoolwork or he won't be able to do it. It takes me a lot of time to talk to his teachers and coordinate his medical appointments. It breaks my day up into fragments so I don't have the time to work. And the other kids deserve attention too.*
A spouse has a history of vocational difficulties: frequent job changes, dismissals, unused education, underemployment or extended unemployment.	*I got fired from my last two jobs about four years ago and now I just do a little computer work for a couple of friends and drive a couple of seniors to their medical appointments. They like having a driver with a Master's degree. I haven't gotten any other job offers.*

Family Law Case Situations That Need a Vocational Evaluation	
Motivation Questions	**Can Sound Like This**
A spouse is working part time but probably has the ability to work full time.	*I am working. I work 15 hours a week in the office and take care of the kids, and supervise their homework, get them to the therapist and the tutor and sports, and chair the school fundraising auction. How much more do you expect me to do?* *I am working. I track the stock market and make all the investment decisions so I read a lot of market information. That takes time. I'm on three Boards of Directors of start-ups. They aren't paid, but I'm spending time researching sources of venture capital. One of them is likely to go further and I expect to be offered a C-level job. I just can't tell when that will happen.*
The supported spouse refuses to go to work.	*I don't think I should have to go to work. We agreed when we got married that I would run the house and raise the kids and I've kept my part of the bargain.*
The supporting spouse has a sudden unexplainable drop in reported earnings.	*You know how hard the industry has been hit lately and the practice just isn't doing as well.*
A spouse's current income is significantly less than in a prior earning period.	*I earned a lot when I was Project Manager at a large corporation but I'm writing a book and thinking about getting into another part of the industry. I need to get exposure to the part of the industry that's growing. My experience is in old technology.*

Family Law Case Situations That Need a Vocational Evaluation	
Career Issues	**Can Sound Like This**
A spouse identifies a vocational goal that seems unrealistic or necessitates a prolonged preparation period.	*I want a different graduate degree, but I'll have to take some prerequisites first and that will take two semesters and then the degree is about 2-3 years, so it'll take about 4 years for me to be ready to look for work.*
A spouse has conducted an extended unsuccessful job search.	*I've been to every networking event I can find, I've called everyone I know. I had three really good prospects and five interviews, but no job offers so far.*
There is disagreement about how much a person can earn.	*When we got married, she had an executive position at a major firm in New York and we were earning the same salary. She's great at her job, just ask any of her bosses. She can earn what she used to earn at her last job.*
A spouse has a self-employment enterprise that is not profitable or not producing sufficient income.	*I have this great line of products that all my friends just love and I sell them from home. I've started making a web site but it's not done yet. I've only done it part time but I could learn about Internet marketing and sell them online, I guess.*

INITIATING A VOCATIONAL EVALUATION

Any of the participants in a litigated family law case can request a vocational evaluation, either singly or jointly. In most cases, the initiators are attorneys who are aware of the usefulness of vocational information and know the Family Code provisions that set up the structure to elicit the information. They are familiar with the local practitioners qualified to perform evaluations and whose testimony will be accepted as expert by the court.

The possible initiators of the vocational evaluation are:

A. A family law attorney representing the supporting spouse, who wants to determine the financial contribution the supported spouse will have to pay in the near term and long term. The attorney engages the cooperation of the supported spouse and his or her attorney to participate in the evaluation. The report in this case goes to the referring attorney, who can share it with the opposing attorney and the court, and use it in negotiating settlement.

If the attorney for the supporting spouse does not want to involve the opposing side, he or she can ask the evaluator to produce data on relevant occupational information, a vocational evaluation with limited services.

B. A family law attorney representing the supported spouse, wanting to ensure the client receives information and advice in meeting his or her obligation to make reasonable efforts to find work or earn income. The report in this case goes to the referring attorney, who may or may not share it with the opposing attorney.

Since the evaluee is initiating the services, the opposing side may not know that the evaluation is occurring unless the supported spouse wants to request the other side share the cost. In that situation, the attorneys cooperate to determine who will pay for the evaluation, or agree to let the court decide.

C. Both attorneys representing the divorcing parties, agreeing informally about the advisability of a vocational evaluation. In this case, the report is sent to both attorneys simultaneously, depending on the arrangements made by agreement.

D. Both attorneys and their clients agreeing formally with a motion to the court requesting a Stipulation and Order for a vocational evaluation. In this case, the report is usually sent to both attorneys simultaneously, although other distribution arrangements can made. In some cases, both spouses are evaluated, either by one evaluator or by separate evaluators for each spouse.

E. The mediator can request that the supported party participate in a vocational evaluation. The report is distributed to the mediator, or to the attorneys and the mediator, according to the communication arrangements agreed among the parties.

F. The Family Court judge or commissioner can order the supported spouse to undergo a vocational examination and appoint an evaluator to function as the Court's expert. In California, this request utilizes the California Evidence Code Section 730.[7] In this case, the evaluator submits the report to the Court and both attorneys simultaneously. The court decides which party/parties pay for the evaluation costs.

G. The supporting party who is unrepresented (*in pro per*) can request a vocational evaluation of the supported spouse without the intervention of an attorney. In this case, the spouse who retains the expert decides on the distribution of the report.

H. The supported party who is unrepresented (*in pro per*) can request a vocational evaluation for himself or herself, usually with vocational counseling and planning, to guide career activities and demonstrate good faith efforts to work toward self-support. In this case, there may not be a report, but if one is written, it is sent to the evaluee/spouse who then decides on its distribution.

DIFFERENCES IN VOCATIONAL EVALUATIONS ACCORDING TO REFERRAL SOURCE AND RETENTION ARRANGEMENTS

When the <u>attorney for the supported spouse refers her own client</u>, both legal strategy and vocational counseling interests prompt the evaluation. The attorney has probably become aware that her client should have vocational planning assistance and wants to have this supportive service from someone she can choose, rather than waiting to have less or no choice in which evaluator will work with her client evaluee.

Alternatively, she may have learned of a difficult vocational and legal issue that will require a sensitive approach, again through an evaluator of her choosing. In this case, she is preemptively taking the initiative in the vocational evaluation rather than waiting until the opposing counsel raises the question of earning capacity.

The major advantages that the referring counsel gains from this move are the choice of evaluator and that the vocational evaluator communicates with the referring attorney solely; as a result, the existence and the results of the vocational evaluation may be unknown, at least initially, to the opposing party and counsel. In this situation, the evaluator may function not as a disclosed retained expert, but as a consultant to the attorney on difficult vocational issues. Only the referring attorney sees the vocational evaluation results, which may be deemed attorney's work product. *Attorney's work product* refers to written case materials that cannot be required to be introduced in court or otherwise revealed to the other side.

For example, the attorney may be aware that her client is very fearful, somewhat fragile, and will require a lot of coaching and time to approach the world of work. The attorney may have real concerns about whether her client can work at all. She may want to initiate the vocational evaluation early in the case when these difficulties become clear in her discussions with her client, to give the client maximal time to work these problems through. She may be looking for an expert opinion on whether the behavior she is seeing is just a temporary or situational response to the divorce, or whether her client is emotionally disabled and will not be able to work at all. If the client is too disabled to work, the attorney will want to think about permanent support and perhaps related complications in custody.

In this situation, the referring attorney may ask for a report or decide she does not want a formal written record with expert conclusions.

The financial obligation for paying for the vocational evaluation in this situation falls on the evaluee, who may see an advantage in choosing the evaluator. Alternately, the evaluee may feel impoverished and not want to spend money to explore a topic – working – that is uncomfortable and unwelcome, even when prompted by the attorney.

The <u>supporting spouse's attorney can refer the evaluee for vocational evaluation</u>; in this situation, the supporting spouse takes the entire financial responsibility for the costs. The evaluee may feel forced into seeing the evaluator. Cooperation, openness in sharing information, and motivation to make changes all can be problematic in this scenario. It is the neutral evaluator's job to help evaluees learn about the benefits of exploring their career options with an employment professional. Whether the evaluee accepts the expert's conclusions or recommendations is not always under the evaluator's control.

As the expert hired by the opposing spouse, the evaluator pays attention to all issues — both those that the attorney feels will strengthen the case and to those that may not. The evaluator may feel it is essential to raise issues that do not suit the attorney's client. This honest evaluation helps the attorney understand positive and negative stands from which to negotiate. It is important to listen to the opposing spouse's viewpoint, but that perspective cannot predetermine the evaluator's conclusions.

In this situation, the evaluator communicates directly with the referring attorney solely, and must be careful not to function, even inadvertently, as the interrogator on behalf of the supporting spouse to catch the evaluee. The evaluator does not have to report every expression of hurt, anger, disappointment, or criticism of the divorcing spouse that the evaluee utters in the natural progression of describing his or her life. These emotions are normal in divorces, but may be unrelated to the vocational outcomes.

However, the evaluator should record relevant statements about noncooperation and lack of motivation to reenter the work world. Contrary to spouses' expectations, expressions of fear, worry, and concern about working are common, but refusals to cooperate motivated by retaliation are rare, especially when the fear of coercion eases in the evaluation.

> **Counselor note:** *In only one instance in thirty years, I heard,*
>
> *I am so angry at my ex. I'm going to do everything I can to make him pay. I'm going to take him to the cleaners. No way am I going to work just so he can pay me less. Why should I?*
>
> *I reminded the evaluee that I was taking notes and would be writing a report. Was she sure she wanted to say that? She repeated it, strongly, and I told her that she should think about it and call me if she changed her mind. She never called and this statement was quoted, verbatim, in my report and in my trial testimony. It affected her support.*
>
> ***NB:*** *in spite of spousal fears that this happens frequently, I have only encountered it once.*

When both attorneys cooperate, either by agreeing informally to a vocational evaluation, or by formalizing the arrangement using a stipulation with a requested court order, to have the supported spouse participate in the vocational evaluation, the evaluator communicates with both attorneys simultaneously. Emails and mail should go to both attorneys; the attorneys and the evaluator should share information about the vocational evaluation in conference calls or face-to-face meetings. Either party's attorney can initiate contact with the evaluator, but both should copy all written communication to opposing counsel. The evaluator and attorney should also share the contents of all phone or in-person conversations with the opposing counsel. The parties may split the cost of the evaluation, or one side may advance the costs or pay them.

When the earning capacity of a spouse clearly becomes an point of contention and the parties and their attorneys cannot agree, the mediator can call in the services of a vocational evaluator. Or the judge or commissioner can initiate a vocational evaluation with the order that the evaluator is the court's expert, invoking Rule of Evidence §730. When the trier of fact asks the expert to function as a source of expert information and opinion under Section 730, the attorneys may not initiate contact with the evaluator, but the evaluator can contact the parties and attorneys freely. The evaluator sends the report to the court with simultaneous copies to both attorneys. The court determines the payor of the evaluation costs.

TIMING THE VOCATIONAL EVALUATION

The basic rule of timing the vocational evaluation is to give the evaluator sufficient time to complete the interviews, testing, data collection, research, and writing that form the content of the summary report. This can take from 30 to 90 days, or longer, depending on the case difficulties, scheduling, and evaluee cooperation. A common period for the evaluation is 45 to 60 days from initial interview (not from the initial call to engage the evaluator) to finished report. The attorney will want to plan long enough that the report arrives well before any court date, settlement conference, or mediation procedure.

This timing focuses on the needs of the attorneys and the evaluator, however. Timing the evaluation to give the evaluee its maximum benefit is also important. The vocational evaluation can start at different points during the months of the divorce to fit the evaluee's requirements. For the evaluee, a vocational evaluation very early in the divorce may be a complex burden, another overwhelming change in a life abruptly filled with change. For others, it is a support structure to settle a major concern.

Because the vocational evaluation can also incorporate career advice, and making emotional shifts and gaining perspective take time, beginning early may offer the evaluee months to make decisions and psychological progress. It takes repetition for some people to hear and adjust to the idea of work, and so to contribute to the vocational conclusions and plan recommendations.

SUGGESTIONS FOR TIMING THE VOCATIONAL EVALUATION

A. Scheduled early in the divorce and attorney consultation, an evaluation gives the evaluee a longer stretch to think about a vocational future, do some vocational exploration without too much time pressure, and adjust to the idea of being a working person.

B. Later in the divorce, the evaluation can occur after the temporary housing changes, schedules for custody, and temporary support have been in place long enough that things feel more settled and less chaotic. Evaluated spouses can then often feel that they have enough control over their lives that they can make personal plans, including work reentry.

C. In a divorce so financially or emotionally complex that it will take a long time to settle, a vocational evaluation started midway can give the evaluee time to begin to implement the career plan. It is especially important if the plan will require a period of building skills or adding education. Using the time of the divorce to implement the career steps will show clear indicators of the potential success of the plan and the likelihood of achieving predicted earnings. If there are doubts about ability to work or motivation to comply, monitoring the spouse's progress and compliance in implementing the plan can occur while settlement issues are active.

D. With an evaluation started after most of the other financial decisions are complete and long-term support is the major outstanding question, a career plan can start immediately and the vocational report can assist in setting expectations for how much the supported spouse can contribute. This is common in a bifurcated divorce, i.e., one in which the issues are separated to be settled at different times, so that the formal divorce is filed even if all the financial matters are not yet settled.

E. The vocational evaluation may come very late in the marital dissolution process, perhaps even after the divorce is final. If support has continued, a vocational evaluation can determine if the supported spouse is making a good faith effort toward employment, or has complied with an agreement or court order to seek work. This may occur at the point when one spouse requests an adjustment or modification in support amounts due to a retirement, change of jobs, or alteration in income.

CAUSES FOR EXTENDED DURATIONS OF AN EVALUATION

- The evaluee's delays, unavailability, or noncooperation with setting, canceling, or keeping appointments.

  I can't come in till after the beginning of next month. I'm too busy.

- Scheduling problems for a busy evaluator.

  I can see you on the tenth, or the twenty-fourth.

- Interruptions caused by major holidays, school vacations, or trips.

  Can we make it after Christmas and New Year's?

- Health issues.

The kids and I all have the flu. I'll call you.

- Delays in getting essential information to form conclusions, such as doctor's reports, acceptance into school programs, or transcripts.

I can't get in to see my doctor for three weeks. I'll bring the forms to you then.

◆ ◆ ◆

Recognizing the signs that essential data are missing in a family law case, and understanding that the answers lie in a vocational evaluation, enable an attorney, a judge, mediator, or one of the parties to call in a vocational expert to expedite the settlement of the divorce.

To find out what one is fitted to do, and to secure an opportunity to do it, is the key to happiness.

Bishop Richard Cumberland

Except for visits to the doctor or a therapist, the interviews connected to the divorce may be the evaluees' first experience answering personal questions from someone outside their intimate circle of family and friends. For some, it is a welcome exploration of their lives with an attentive professional; for people who are normally very selective about those with whom they share private information, it may feel invasive. In divorce, the disclosure of financial, emotional, and other family matters can be disquieting to the divorcing spouses. This is especially true when parties are aware that material information can become part of court records and thus be publicly available.

Family matters, money, health, and other personal details are all standard topics in vocational counseling practice in many venues, including divorce. The outline below can help attorneys and evaluees know what the structured vocational interview will cover, so they are not surprised by the questions or by the expectation of discussing their lives. If evaluees have concerns about the relevance of inquiries in their vocational evaluations, they should always question the evaluator about why a specific personal detail is necessary and important.

WHAT HAPPENS IN THE VOCATIONAL EVALUATION

To engage the cooperation of the evaluee, the opposing spouse, and the attorneys, it is wise to explain the vocational evaluation process. This often reduces fear and delays.

ACTIVITY	PURPOSE	RESULTS
STRUCTURED INTERVIEW	Explain vocational process Collect basic information Diagnose vocational assets and deficits and motivation influences Identify transferable skills	Essential knowledge of evaluee Evaluee involvement in evaluation outcome Evaluee assignments for self-assessment and information
VOCATIONAL TESTING	Obtain objective measurements of interests, skills, aptitudes, achievements, and work values	Confirmed transferable skills Potential vocational alternatives
IDENTIFICATION of VOCATIONAL OPTIONS	Interpret test results and consider evaluee feedback Consolidate subjective and objective findings to identify viable vocational options	Specific job titles for vocational exploration Increased evaluee self-awareness and self-confidence Assignments for evaluee research activities
LABOR MARKET RESEARCH	Explore job availability, current and potential wages, entry methods for selected jobs in appropriate geographic area	Up-to-date data used to determine earning capacity
EARNING CAPACITY ANALYSIS & REPORT	Summarize individual earning capacity, integrating evaluee background and labor market conditions	Objective, verifiable expert opinion of earning capacity, ability and opportunity to work
VOCATIONAL RECOMMENDATIONS	Outline activities, resources, costs, and timing to achieve vocational goal	Clear, concise individualized career plan to reach maximal employment

COMPONENTS OF A VOCATIONAL EVALUATION

The Family Law Code sections that specify areas of concern can be one influence on the contents of the vocational evaluation. The expert evaluation for the court offers an estimate of what the evaluee can earn and when earnings will occur so that the trier of fact can compare it to the marital standard of living. The court or those trying to settle the case need to know what the party's marketable skills are, if the individual requires a vocational plan to acquire updated or new marketable skills, and what the expenses and time for this plan will be.

The law establishes the requirement for the transferable ("marketable") skills assessment gleaned from educational and experiential histories, supplemented with optional testing, and the development of a vocational plan and its details including sources for training or skill development, their duration, and costs.

These provisions also set the requirement to consider the needs of the children, including their health conditions, in planning the custodial parents' vocational lives. Also considered are the age and health of the evaluee and their impact, if any, on future work.

The methods of performing vocational assessments also derive from the long history of the profession of vocational rehabilitation counseling and its related field, career counseling. Vocational rehabilitation first began formally as a method of helping returning World War I soldiers readjust to work after experiencing injuries. It developed into an internationally recognized professional field of study to assist people with any physical or psychological barriers to entry or reentry into the workplace. With the increasing sophistication of the profession, standard assessment topics developed.

The list of report contents below will familiarize the court, evaluees, and their attorneys with what they can expect in a vocational evaluation report and will inform the evaluee about the range of topics they will encounter in the assessment interview.

CONTENTS OF A FAMILY LAW VOCATIONAL EVALUATION REPORT

These standard topics in vocational evaluation reports can be modified and others can be added as necessary.

In the report section often titled **BACKGROUND**, the evaluator describes the evaluee's age and social situation. These factors, which can influence vocational planning, include family members and childcare responsibilities, family expectations or businesses that might be a resource for training, employment, or work contacts. The number and age of the children and their schooling are often reported along with the custody schedule to clarify work availability.

The family's location, commute times, and available transportation, if they will influence the parent's work choices, are discussed.

The evaluee's **EDUCATION** is a summary with some detail about educational experiences, formal and informal, including schools attended, degrees, certificates, and self-education. In this section, frequent school changes, lack of success in academic subjects, or problems with academics may point to learning differences or difficulties. These details create the understanding of the need for any educational remediation or accommodations in a career plan to ameliorate the negative effect of vocational barriers on occupational choice.

The education discussion can reveal other life experiences that can influence the evaluee's work life. For instance, for a person whose family moved so often that the evaluee never really learned arithmetic, taking a basic course in math can close this learning gap, or instead can point the evaluee toward avoiding jobs that do not require calculating, as a way to accommodate it. An evaluee who spent high school avoiding a dysfunctional family by drinking and using drugs may not have learned much during this essential part of schooling, a situation that can explain the gaps in some knowledge or lack of a college degree. The vocational plan can address this issue if it has a long-term vocational implication.

In the **EXPERIENCE** section, the list of the evaluee's vocational and avocational experiences demonstrates the full range of the evaluee's skills, knowledge, and abilities. These experiences include work, volunteering, internships, hobbies, part-time work, freelance projects, and work within family businesses, paid or unpaid. Details such as job titles, dates of employment, how the evaluee found each job and the reason for leaving it, salaries and other compensation, promotions, and work relationships help guide future career thoughts.

The **HEALTH** section of the report contains a description of the evaluee's physical and mental health if these will influence work hours, job choices, or other occupational concerns. For many, if not most people, this section will be very short, to indicate that the evaluator addressed the topic, or omitted if the evaluee has no health conditions related to work. If health problems exist, this section describes any influences on vocational capacity. Recent daily activities help the evaluator understand the functional capacity of the evaluee.

A description of the evaluee's thoughts about **VOCATIONAL GOALS** contains any expressed interests, desires, and contemplated vocational activities and plans. Even if these are tentative, possibly unrealistic, or unlikely to succeed, it is important for the evaluator to listen to the evaluee's initial thoughts and not set them aside preemptively. If they will not work, the evaluator gives reasons for dismissing an evaluee's initially proposed job idea.

VOCATIONAL TESTING describes any formal evaluation using published tests, with a description of the test and the evaluee's scores compared to the proper norm group. Individualized vocational testing can look at skills, aptitudes, interests, personality, values, reading ability, learning ability, or other job-related attributes. The counselor's interpretation explains the use of the scores in career planning. For instance, high verbal comprehension and word fluency scores will help support a career plan using oral/verbal skills in sales, public relations, or web content creation. Testing is tailored to the person; not all evaluees need testing.

The inclusion of focused **LABOR MARKET RESEARCH** supplies recent information about job availability, salary and requirements from published data, employers, and industry experts, keyed to the industry and geographic location.

The evaluator's **VOCATIONAL CONCLUSIONS** are expert opinions about employability, recommended occupations, earning capacity, wages, with demonstrable job openings, or other evidence of employment opportunities.

The **VOCATIONAL PLAN**, if one is necessary and requested, details one or more vocational plans including duration, costs, training resources and their program details and content, and probable jobs for which the plan will qualify the evaluee.

If appropriate, the report may have an **ASSESSMENT OF THE JOB SEARCH EFFORTS** of an evaluee who is expected, and perhaps ordered by the Court, to be hunting for work.

CONCLUSIONS IN THE VOCATIONAL EVALUATION

The vocational evaluator summarizes his or her expert opinions in the **CONCLUSIONS** section of the vocational report. The conclusions from the evaluation will address the evaluee's ability to work and identify any limitations that would modify the default assumption that a person can work full time. See Chapter 6 for a longer discussion of the issues of health.

The conclusions can summarize the vocational assets – skills, aptitudes, knowledge, experience, and resources – and any vocational barriers. They may also describe personality dynamics, interests, geography, and other influences on career choice. These elements establish the foundation for the suggested vocational options.

In the conclusions, the evaluator may list multiple career scenarios that fit the evaluee. For example, one job option might generate income more quickly but bring in a lower salary; another could require a longer preparation time to reenter the labor market but would be more likely to yield a higher income in the long term. The evaluator may recommend which option will work better for the evaluee, and why, or leave this decision to the evaluee. To reach these conclusions, the evaluator will research the labor market to find evidence that jobs similar to those the evaluee will seek are available in sufficient quantity that the evaluee will be offered employment. The labor market research will also supply estimates of earnings at various points in the evaluee's career, both at entry and with some experience. See Chapter 8 for a discussion of labor market research.

The conclusions address self-employment if this topic was part of the considered options. See Chapter 5 for a longer discussion. The evaluator may opine about the viability of a self-employment or career plan and show specific data to underpin the opinion.

If the evaluee is not already pursuing a career path, the evaluator can outline the details of the steps to a proposed job title and the anticipated duration of the plan. The conclusions may list training options with recommendations, projected costs, duration, and certificate or degree sought.

If the evaluee could benefit from post-evaluation career services to support the implementation of vocational plan, it is important to clarify whether the career counselor will be asked later to report on the evaluee's participation. The career counseling that follows an evaluation is usually private, meant to assist the evaluee to succeed in the plan. If the attorneys also intend to use the career counseling to monitor the evaluee's compliance with the plan, the privacy aspects of the counseling relationship change. The attorneys or the court may anticipate that the counselor will report in a year or two about contacts with the evaluee, what she was asked to do and whether she completed those assignments, and whether she made a good faith effort to find work or finish a school program. Either way, the expectation should be explicit.

If the focus of the evaluation is on an assessment of the evaluee's current work and earnings, a career plan will not be part of the conclusions. Instead, an analysis of the evaluee's efforts to find work or to earn income is a major section of the conclusions. If the evaluee is conducting a job search or has received a court order to seek work, the adequacy of the effort – sufficient time spent, effectiveness of activities and contacts, breadth of outreach, suitability of the resume and cover letters – may be assessed. The evaluator may suggest changes in the job search and resources for more effective job hunting. See Chapter 5 on assessing the adequacy of job search efforts.

ACCOMMODATIONS IN THE VOCATIONAL EVALUATION

To accommodate diverse evaluees, the evaluator can modify the vocational evaluation process. Because the methodology of the evaluation should remain as consistent as possible, the evaluator should only make changes to assist evaluees needing accommodations.

LOCATION

The norm for vocational evaluations is that the evaluee keeps appointments with the evaluator in his or her office setting. The meeting's location can be changed for a good reason but should not be changed arbitrarily. A disabled evaluee may need to meet in a setting closer to home to avoid excessive travel that would exacerbate physical or mental illnesses. If the evaluator services a large territory, he or she may have to travel and use a temporary office, a conference room, or even the evaluee's own home to conduct the interview. A neutral setting, outside the home if possible, is preferable.

When the divorce is exceptionally hostile, one party's attorney may request that the interview take place in the attorney's office. This is not ideal, as the setting is not a neutral one, the attorney may ask to be present, and the locale can influence the openness of the evaluee's responses.

If the evaluee requests that the evaluator travel to the meeting to save the evaluee time or effort, the evaluee should bear the cost of the evaluator's travel time. A preferable alternative is that the evaluator explains that the structured interviews and testing normally take place in the evaluator's office where all the information and testing materials are available and the setting is neutral. This helps the evaluation methodology to remain consistent.

RECORDING

The interview between the evaluator and evaluee can be recorded if necessary. Occasionally the evaluee or one of the attorneys asks to record the evaluation. This may reflect a lack of trust or a major conflict between the parties, where the suspicions extend to all parts of the divorce. In this situation, the evaluator should request a signed document that states that person doing the recording will give an exact unedited copy of the recording or video to the evaluator within a reasonable time. The recording technology should not interfere with the free exchange of information between the evaluator and evaluee by being intrusive, dominant in the room, noisy or technically disturbing.

The vocational testing should definitely not be recorded, however. Recording the testing process[8] alters the carefully defined methodology of the test publisher and can render the testing invalid as a result. It also can violate the evaluator's agreement as a purchaser of the test publisher's products to maintain the confidentiality of the test instruments. One test publisher's website (PAR, Inc.) describes this requirement: "test instruments are trade secrets and protected by intellectual property laws including copyright and trade secret laws, and their usefulness and value would be greatly compromised if they were generally available to the public."

Another reason for recording the evaluation is to accommodate an evaluee with a disability or one who has difficulty understanding English. For people whose hearing makes it hard for them to be certain they have understood the interview questions, a recording is a reasonable accommodation. For evaluees with auditory processing disorders who have difficulty understanding oral input, or those with attention or memory problems, or those who want to remember the interview without being able to take written notes, a recording may also be a welcome accommodation. Such accommodations are mandated by the Federal Americans with

Disabilities Act (ADA) and by state and local laws. In California, the nondiscrimination law for people with disabilities is the Fair Employment and Housing Act (FEHA).

Vocational experts generally accept that audio recordings do not present a difficulty in the vocational evaluation, as they are usually unobtrusive and do not materially change the nature of the exchange between the evaluator and evaluee. Video recordings are much more intrusive and difficult to ignore, and may make the evaluee reluctant to discuss topics freely and candidly.

The general principle about recordings is to alter the standard evaluation methodology as little as possible and only for an essential reason, to maintain consistency, and ensure reliability and validity.

ATTENDEES

While the evaluation is not confidential and its contents are in the written report, the evaluator usually interviews the evaluee alone, or sometimes with professional assistants. It is possible to add others to the conversation, but additional persons should attend only when their presence is necessary to make the evaluation possible and effective.

Interpreters or translators are practical additions to the interview when the evaluee's language skills are insufficient to make it possible to convey the subtle details that explain a person's background. The interpreter or translator who shares culture as well as language with the evaluee can be especially effective. Their cultural knowledge can explain the evaluee's educational background, cultural norms, and idiomatic language. For instance, a translator can help describe how many years of school are normal for children in another country, or how an evaluee's upbringing reflects normal expectations for young people in that culture.

In some situations, children of immigrants use their English skills to function as intermediaries for their parents in their daily life. Children should usually not be the translators for divorcing evaluees in vocational evaluations, as the topics may concern parental disputes, money, fears, and worries that are not suitable to share with a child.

Adult family members or friends sometimes sit in if they are needed. For instance, if an evaluee has difficulty discussing her or his life, a person who knows her or him well can assist in the evaluator's understanding. Possible functions for a support person in the room are to take notes, run a recording device, or reduce anxiety. In general, however, someone who drives the evaluee to the meeting or accompanies him or her for support waits outside the meeting for him or her to finish. Sometimes parents who have not arranged childcare bring children to the evaluation. Young children who cannot understand the conversation may be permitted to stay if they do not distract the parent's attention, but the presence of older children can constrain the parent's ability to be candid. Children's attendance at the meeting should be discouraged as the offices are not child proofed and office staff should not be asked to function as babysitters.

If the evaluee's attorney wants to witness the evaluation, the meetings can be modified to permit this. It is essential that the primary information come from the evaluee, however, not from anyone else in attendance. The evaluator should caution anyone who joins the interview not to prompt the evaluee, speak for him or her, or interfere with the information flow. The report should note the presence of anyone else in the room, along with any change in the procedure caused by this extra presence.

If a case assistant, intern, or graduate student is part of the vocational evaluator's staff, the evaluator should ask permission of the evaluee to allow the assistant's attendance in the interview.

LIMITED VOCATIONAL EVALUATIONS

In some situations, it is reasonable to conduct only parts of the vocational evaluation methodology. For some people asking about a vocational evaluation, the first consideration is that of cost, with the idea that is would be less expensive to answer a single vocational question. This is a common request from divorcing spouses acting as their own attorneys *in pro per*. This does not always achieve the actual outcome the spouse wants, but sometimes it can work well.

Of the three essential vocational evaluation services — earning capacity evaluation, labor market research, and vocational planning — the labor market research component is the most obvious vocational service to stand alone.

Vocational counseling is also a separable service. Vocational counseling while someone is divorcing is not an evaluation; its results are personal and not intended for use in the litigation. The conclusions and process can be kept confidential, a key distinction from a vocational evaluation that is part of the litigation, where a major intent is to share the decisions made in the discussions between the counselor and evaluee. It is important to distinguish between these two types of services from the beginning – confidential career planning versus vocational counseling to be reported in a vocational evaluation – because the counseling evaluee should be able to decide what confidential information to reveal or not before the interview starts.

One type of limited evaluation is labor market research on job availability and salaries only, based on the details in a resume or list of past jobs without an interview with the evaluee whose career is the subject of research. This is an option if the evaluee refuses to cooperate, if there is no court order to compel participation in the evaluation, or if one side wants to collect information without the knowledge of the other party or attorney.

Without a personal interview, the referring party or the attorney must supply the essential information about the job and the person who is the subject of the research.

A limited vocational evaluation for labor market research can be useful if the evaluator knows the important elements of the evaluee's work-related situation. The referring spouse and attorney must be careful to offer all the facts, though there is often an inclination to disclose only those that help support their side of the case. Labor market research alone is very informative if it accurately describes potential working conditions for a litigant, but it has no value in enlightening the judge who is deciding support if it ignores relevant employability influences such as long separation from the labor market, the existence of a disability, or the erosion of marketable skills through disuse. Such a report is not credible and it may not be neutral.

Limited vocational evaluations often answer questions like these:

- How much can a person earn with 5 years of experience in *[fill in job title]* in the geographic area reached with a normal commute?

- Do applicants entering this career need a degree or a certificate?

- How many hours do people in *[fill in job title]* normally work each week in this part of the state?

- Are jobs available for people with *x* years of recent experience as a *[fill in job title]?*

Example A) The supported wife is already working in a career she chose and is willing to continue in; the supporting ex-husband is unsure that she is earning as much or as many hours as is standard in the current market.

My wife is only working 32 hours a week. She says that's normal for everyone in the medical profession. I work more than 40 hours per week and I think that is what most people do. Why should I support her if she's only working part time and I'm the one working more than full time? What are the standard hours for my wife's medical profession?

The supporting spouse wants to know what the standard work hours and pay rates for this occupation are in a defined geographic location. He may also want to know if it is reasonable to expect her to get a better-paying job if she leaves her position. A focused labor market report can present those answers. This can also clarify the question of whether a supporting spouse is earning up to capacity.

Example B) Husband wants to move to out of state and still to share frequent custody of the children, which would require the working ex-wife to move too. Wife says, *"No, I can't move to Atlanta. There are no jobs for me there."* Is that true? Are jobs for her skill set available in the Atlanta area? A labor market can answer the question, using the knowledge of the ex-wife's education, experience, work history, and areas of expertise.

Example C) Ex-husband is working in a computer tech field and has a certificate in a networking and systems administration but no college degree. The ex-wife feels that he could earn more if he had a different job that used this certification he earned recently. Is he qualified for other jobs? What job titles do his skills qualify him to get? Do they really pay more than he is now earning? Are they available to him in this market although he has no degree? Labor market research is the appropriate service to request. Well-defined, it will encompass the germane queries: whether the job openings exist, what skills and education employers are requiring, what average compensation ranges are.

A limited vocational evaluation is not as useful, however, where a spouse has not been working or has not developed vocational interests, or where health questions of either the spouse or the child may appear. The vocational evaluator should point out that the limited vocational exploration will only raise further questions.

The vocational evaluator should have complete, accurate, and recent information and all the important facts about the supported spouse whose career details she or he is researching. Otherwise, the conclusion she or he reaches may not apply to the facts of the case. If the parties have already lived separately for months or years, the spouse requesting the limited vocational evaluation may have only an old resume to give to the researcher. Questions of pay, job availability and opportunity, and candidates' qualifications for a position are specific in the minds of employers. To make the labor market analyses valid and reliable, the underlying facts must also be specific and complete. In the situations below, a limited vocational evaluation will not suffice.

A divorcing party who walks into court and tells the judge, *"My ex can earn $39,000 a year and I have an expert report that says so"* may be confronted with other details that make the report irrelevant, making the report with a limited scope a waste of money.

For instance, if the vocational evaluator does not know that ex-spouse has additional work experience or education, the research may have little relevance to actual conditions considered by the trier of fact. The judge or opposing attorney or evaluee may say:

Yes, you have data showing that medical secretaries earn about $39,000 per year, but did you inform the vocational evaluator that the respondent has only one more semester to finish a degree in computer science and certificates in networking? The pay scale for computer networkers is the important number we need now, and this research does not give us that information.

The job openings and pay rates you are showing don't apply to the work I've actually done. These are for people who have corporate experience with international businesses. I've never worked for large companies like these. The job titles are the same but the job duties are completely different.

◆ ◆ ◆

With an established methodology that underlies the assessment, vocational evaluations are flexible and can accommodate the individual situations for diverse evaluees.

CHAPTER FIVE — ASSESSING EARNING CAPACITY

I have a liking for honest work, and honest work as I see it is work that is done for the worker's enjoyment as much as for the profit it will bring him. And henceforth that's my work.

Dashiell Hammett, author of *The Maltese Falcon,* in a letter to his editor

Dashiell Hammett's "honest work" can refer not just to a vocational counselor's fascination with how people fit into the numerous varieties of work, but also to the approach counselors bring to the development of vocational conclusions about vocational choice and earning capacity.

In Alice in Wonderland (Carroll, 1923), Alice asks the Cheshire Cat, "Would you tell me, please, which way I ought to walk from here?" "That depends a good deal on where you want to get to," said the Cat. The Cheshire Cat sounds as if he's starting the vocational planning process, by helping Alice define her goals before she decides on her path. Vocational counselors outside of Wonderland will ask further questions to gather the important information for career planning.

EARNING CAPACITY OF EVALUEES WHO ARE NOT WORKING

Since earning capacity is specific both to the individual and to his or her position in the work world, generic assumptions about the person's potential earnings can over- or underestimate earning power. For a nonworking evaluee without a job goal, the first evaluation step is determining job titles on which to build a vocational plan. The assessment uses career planning methods similar to those used in a non-litigated setting to create credible and useful vocational goals.

Beyond education and work history, including the period of separation from the labor market, other factors can be influential in guiding career choice and potentially necessary training, among them these:

- Interests

- Cultural background and expectations

- Language skills

- Availability of financial resources

- Geography and transportation

- Personality traits such as organization, decision making, sociability, communication skills, and others

- Hiring biases and trends of the industry

- Existence of a non-compete agreement, revoked licenses, legal problems or other legal constraints on job choice

Several of these factors rise to major importance and are frequent topics in vocational evaluations.

THE QUESTION OF INTERESTS

In career decisions, the question of a person's interests is always a concern, and it is reasonable to pay attention to interests in exploring vocational aspirations. Whether interests should be the primary determinant of a career goal, or the only one, has been a matter of debate in many venues. When the California legislature attempted to omit interests as a factor for vocational plans for injured workers receiving vocational rehabilitation through workers' compensation insurance, the vocational counseling community successfully lobbied to reinsert interests as an essential component of career planning.

Interests are not discrete aspects of an individual's personality. They are linked to work and nonwork activities, aptitudes and developed skills, and personal values. Many interest assessment instruments, such as the frequently administered Strong Interest Inventory (CPP, Inc. 1994), recognize these connections. The Strong test structure uses six categories (the Holland codes) to describe potential interest areas in the work world.

Artistic interests are associated with values such as appreciation of beauty, originality, independence, and imagination, and use skills like creativity, and musical or artistic expression.

Conventional interests direct individuals toward organization, data management, accounting, investing, and information systems, performing activities using procedures, records, and computer applications. Working with numbers, data, finances, and other details are skills used by those who value accuracy, stability, and efficiency.

Enterprising interests focus on business, politics, leadership and entrepreneurship, connected to risk taking, status, competition, and influence. Activities in this area —selling, managing, persuading, and marketing, among others — require skills such as verbal ability, ability to motivate and direct others.

Investigative interests center on science, medicine, mathematics and research for those with skills and aptitudes in math, analysis, and writing. Values such as independence, curiosity, and learning are connected to Investigative work.

Realistic interests point toward work operating machines and using tools, building, repairing, athletic activity, and working outdoors for those with mechanical ingenuity, dexterity, physical coordination. Values associated with Realistic jobs are tradition, practicality, and common sense.

Social interests link to values of cooperation, generosity, and service to others, and lead to activities such as teaching, counseling, training, and caring for others. People skills, verbal ability, listening skills, and showing understanding are applicable.

With interests so deeply embedded in personality structure, basing a career on them taps into the evaluee's strengths, and elicits enthusiasm and willing cooperation.

Interests alone do not govern career choice and guarantee job fit, however. Successful career choice depends on the interrelation between the individual and the actual world of work. Employers have legitimate needs and structure their job requirements to fulfill these needs. Paying attention only to an individual's interests without awareness of the realities of the world of work and employers' requirements can lead to unrealizable aspirations, dreams rather than goals, and frustration accompanied by low income. On the other hand, paying attention solely to the labor market side, that is, only to which employers are hiring and paying most, is likely to result in job dissatisfaction and frequent job changes.

> Planning careers solely on the individual's interest preferences, can lead to unrealizable aspirations, dreams rather than goals, and frustration accompanied by low income.
>
> Paying attention exclusively to the labor market, however, only to which employers are hiring and paying most, is likely to result in job dissatisfaction, less than optimal performance, and frequent job changes.

In family law vocational evaluations, the evaluator looks for expressions of interest in the evaluee's self-description, strengths in education, choices and successes in experiences, choices of hobbies, and through testing. Tapping into interests is a strong first step in making career choices, but interests that do not translate well into income production often need modification or expansion.

Many workers enjoy a variety of tasks but do not rank one set above others. Others have difficulty choosing only one career path. For some people, the satisfactions of a job lie in working with people they like or in doing a job well and receiving appreciation, rather than in performing a type of career task or function. For them, finding the right setting and compatible coworkers are more important than pursuing a particular interest.

Functioning as counselors, evaluators try to listen positively to the ideas about work suggested by evaluees. Sometimes it is obvious to the experienced counselor that an idea will not be productive, though that is not clear to the evaluee. Talking ideas through with the person allows them to see where snags will arise. It is important for the evaluator not to dismiss suggestions preemptively, even those that immediately sound impractical, without some discussion. Balancing respect for the evaluee's proposed jobs with an expert understanding of the work world and its remuneration possibilities is an essential, though delicate, part of the vocational evaluation.

> *I'm writing a novel. I'm through the first draft and I'm looking for an agent. I love to write and I want to make my living writing fiction. I can even publish it online.*

> *I'm an artist and it's very important to me to be able to express my creativity in whatever I do. I'm willing to be flexible about work but I can't stand the idea of sitting in front of a computer all day.*

> *My faith has become a strong focus in my life and I want to study at the theological center. I could be a minister or work with people in trouble through my church. I think people need to grow spiritually. I've started to take a weekly class, but I don't know what it would take to get accepted into an actual program to become ordained.*

> *I want to work with animals. I volunteer at the Marine Mammal Center. No, I don't have a degree in biology, I just love the animals.*

Working with evaluees who have difficulty in making decisions, evaluators have the task of assisting the person to gather sufficient information to make a choice without letting the evaluation drag on unreasonably, or truncating it prematurely.

For those who are not interested in work, or at least in activities that create an income, the concept of imputed income applies. This attribution of potential income allows the spouse who chooses not to work to be self-determining and follow his or her interests, but prevents him or her from imposing the financial burdens of this choice on the other spouse. More on this in Chapter 9.

The vocational evaluator can offer alternatives to the trier of fact by laying out two or more scenarios for an evaluee's vocational future. One can be the evaluee's first choice with its likely earnings projection. Another can describe another job title, perhaps less interesting to the evaluee but one that could be available sooner or offer higher earnings. The description of each option should describe the correlation with the evaluee's interests as well as potential earnings, time to achieve the vocational target, and the methods to reach it.

The evaluator does not choose the evaluee's vocational options, but can make suggestions. The evaluator does not determine the imputed earnings amount; that is the responsibility of the trier of fact. But the evaluator is an expert in vocational assessment and can reasonably express an expert opinion on which vocational option has a likelihood of success, which is more attainable, which career plan has a shorter time frame or a higher earning outcome. The expert opinion should be based on data in the report; the trier of fact decides on the strength of that evidence how much to rely on the expert's conclusions.

The vocational counseling part of evaluations often feels like a very positive step, an unexpected benefit during a difficult time in the evaluee's life.

Thank you for your help in helping me figuring this all out. Your advice has given me a clearer lens to see how to approach this next stage of my life and helped loosen the financial cobra around my neck.

The vocational planning is the thing that is hopeful in my life right now. Everything else is stress.

TIME OUT OF THE LABOR MARKET

Many vocational evaluees are reentering work after a significant period of being out of the labor market. The diminution of skills, lack of current knowledge in the field, and detachment from networks of colleagues are all factors to consider in assessing the earning capacity, employer acceptability, and likely job hunt duration for a reentry worker.

Spouses who remember the early careers of their ex-partners may have difficulty accepting the difference an employment gap makes in how the labor market will greet resumes with no work history for a multi-year period.

She was a well-respected professional in our field and earned a lot of money when we met. She had a corner office! Everyone loved her. I think all she needs to do is get back in touch with her old colleagues and they'll welcome her back, maybe even as a VP which she was before. I know she's been out of it for nine years, but she still has some friends in the business. There's no reason she shouldn't just move back into a job like the one she had.

Although some evaluees are fearful that no employer will want them, hiring managers frequently hear about gaps in employment. They care about causes for the gaps as much as the fact of the break in employment. It is the job seeker's task, with possible help from the evaluator or a trainer in job seeking skills, to learn how to describe the intervening period since she or he last worked. By helping the employer understand the reasons for the time away from work, the job applicant conveys not only her chronological history, but also her efforts to maintain her skills, volunteer activities, and the personal and professional traits she still brings to a new position.

Reentry into some fields is as simple as taking a refresher course in, say, computer software, and then applying to employers. For others, returning to a field after a significant absence is more daunting, and sometimes impossible. For instance, for a physician who has not treated a patient in a dozen years, his knowledge of current medications, electronic record-keeping, medically related laws, and new diagnostic and treatment technology all need updating. He will be in competition with recent medical school graduates who can prove they are current in all these aspects of modern medical care. If the equivalent experience of a residency year is not available to the returning physician, few hospitals and physician groups will be willing to take the risk of insuring his work while he gains current hands-on experience. For this MD, returning to treating patients may not be an alternative or an immediate reentry option. The evaluator explores other work using his degree and background.

For a salesperson, a major asset to a future employer may be the book of business and network of professional contacts she brings. A break in employment, with no book of business to offer as a result, may make reemployment in the same role a nonstarter for this jobseeker. She may need to return to the industry in a different role, or take a sales position in which she does not need to bring business to be welcomed.

Researchers found that when they reenter the work force, reentry women's wages commonly lag behind those of women at comparable stages in their careers who did not leave the labor force. These data were collected almost twenty years ago (Jacobsen and Levin, 1995), and it is not known whether they apply equally to men who reenter work, if additional training mitigates the difference, or if the technology economy has changed compensation levels and patterns. Researchers found that after some time at work, the wages tended to rebound and the wage differential diminished with years of work.

Jacobsen and Levin (1995) explain this difference:

First, women who leave the labor force and later reenter do not build up seniority, which, by itself, often leads to higher wages. Second, women who return to the labor force are less likely to receive on-the-job training to increase their productivity and thereby raise their pay. Third, when women are not in the work force, their job skills may depreciate. Finally, employers may view gaps in work history as a signal that women who leave may do so again. Some employers would therefore hire them for less important, lower-paying jobs to limit the impact of a future decision to leave.

Many evaluees need to add skills to reenter the workplace. This is particularly true in times of high unemployment when employers have many qualified applicants from whom to choose and do not need to offer on-the-job training to a new hire. The basic functions of skill training are to add recent experience to the jobseeker's resume and increase his or her confidence, but it has additional benefits. Being in a structured program also allows the reentry worker to get used to working within a defined schedule, meeting deadlines, achieving to another's standards, and coordinating family life with activity outside the home. Since school programs are often less than full time, adding training to child rearing schedules functions as a period of adjusting to work, without the threat of losing a job for less than perfect performance.

Understanding, researching, and explaining the financial consequences of the career interruption are important tasks for the vocational evaluator. It is important to insert skill building and work adjustment into a vocational plan when they are needed, and equally important not to allow the evaluee's fears about work reentry to extend the plan unduly.

EARNING CAPACITY OF EVALUEES WHO ARE SEEKING WORK

Fie upon this quiet Life! I want work.

William Shakespeare, *King Henry IV*

If the party in a divorce has realistically defined a job goal or set of related job titles, development of a target for the job search is less essential. If there is doubt about the realism of the choice, the evaluator may compare the career goals with the labor market to confirm the viability of the chosen job title. Once it is clear that job opportunity and appropriate skills coexist, focus in the evaluation shifts from vocational counseling to understanding the party's job search and assessing whether he or she is doing enough to find work.

THE LEGAL REQUIREMENT TO SEEK WORK

The California courts have stated (Morrison, 1978), that "it certainly may be inferred that … the Legislature intended that all who were able to do so should seek employment."

The Gavron (CA 1988) case recognized that before support can be changed, a spouse should "be made aware of the obligation to become self-supporting" with "reasonable advance warning that after an appropriate period of time the supported spouse was expected to become self-sufficient or face onerous legal and financial consequences." In California, the notice to the party that she or he is expected to find work is called a "Gavron warning."

Following Gavron (1988), the courts can issue "orders encouraging supported spouses to seek employment and to work toward becoming self-supporting." These orders, known in California as "Seek Work Orders", require documentation of activities aimed at finding work. The Seek Work Form for documenting job search activities is in Appendix G.

If the subject of a Seek Work Order is not working and spousal support levels are in question, a vocational evaluator can analyze how well the evaluee is conducting his or her job search, whether the efforts are sufficient, effective, and consistent, and why he or she is not yet successful in finding a job.

The preliminary assumption is that the job hunter has the skills required by employers for jobs that are available. If that is not the case, vocational counseling, not job hunt assessment, is the next step.

Using expert knowledge about job search in the labor market, the evaluator assesses whether the job seeker is conducting an effective job search. The job seeker has the responsibility to document his or her efforts and, if personal interviews are possible, to supplement written materials with a description of what he or she has been doing to find work. The vocational report can detail the efforts, estimate how long it should take the job searcher to find work, and suggest supplemental techniques for more effective job hunting.

If the job search is not yet successful, although the evaluee should have been able to get a job offer with his or her existing work skills, the vocational evaluation report analyzes the evaluee's good faith in the attempts toward becoming self-supporting and what further efforts, if any, are necessary to make the job search fruitful. Earnings can be imputed and support changed if the job seeker is deliberately putting less than needed effort into job search. Job search guidelines for comparison to job seekers' efforts are in Appendix H.

ASSESSING GOOD FAITH JOB SEARCH EFFORTS

Warning job hunters that they are expected both to look for work and to record their job search activities assists them in understanding the court's expectations, but many people returning to work need more detailed advice.

To help people who have not developed job search skills or need to learn effective techniques for using new technology for employment, instructing them on what job search activities are more or less successful is a practical part of the vocational evaluation. Providing job search guidelines, such as those listed in Appendix H, has two functions: the instructions teach the job seeker what to do, and the guidelines establish a measurable standard for comparison to actual job search activity if it is necessary to assess whether the job seeker acted in good faith. If the job seeker is not working within a reasonable period even though she or he has had guidance in job hunting, the presence of job search guidelines can help demonstrate that the job search efforts were insufficient or other barriers to employment exist.

The basic answer to the question of how much job search is enough is until you find a job but this is too simplistic a response, especially in a difficult economy such as the one existing as this is written in 2012. Job searches are currently extending to ten months or more, a daunting prospect for someone who faces employer unresponsiveness and frequent rejection. Jobseekers at the end of 2010 had to double the median number of weeks they sought work, in comparison to the number of weeks unemployed jobseekers in 2007 needed to find work. (Ilg, 2011)

Job hunting should be the major weekday activity of a serious job seeker, 20 to 30 hours per week according to common recommendations of vocational professionals.

Job search time includes preparatory activities such as writing a resume and a model cover letter, informational interviewing, researching on the Internet, and practicing interview answers. It is also valuable to spend time keeping records of job search efforts and reviewing what is, and is not, working. These preparatory activities often feel less scary, but cannot be a substitute for reaching out into the real world. The most valuable activity in job search is making personal contacts by networking, either face-to-face, by phone, or via email.

For job seekers who are intimidated by the expectation that they should be able to explain why they are out of work, the easiest way to job hunt is to submit an application online and thus avoid personal interactions. Unfortunately, this method is often the least successful way to look for work, as it places the job seeker into the largest and most competitive pool of applicants, with little hope of being distinguished from the crowd. Some career experts estimate that only two to five percent of jobs are filled through online applications.

Perhaps the most important success factor in job search is putting in enough time. There is no single standard for the number of hours, or applications, for success, but it is common to see job searching itself called a full time job. The Bureau of Labor Statistics (Jones, 2004) says, "Jobseekers should spend a significant amount of time networking." In the unpublished Magruder case (CA 2008), the trial court ordered Mr. Magruder to submit applications for eight jobs a week, after he had failed to secure work over a period of several months. Family Code section 3558 says that a parent who defaults on a child support obligation can be compelled to seek employment when necessary to meet that obligation. The parent may be asked to demonstrate compliance to the court every two weeks with a list of at least five different places the parent has applied for employment. However, courts are not usually this specific about what constitutes a good faith job search. More commonly, courts mandate "best efforts" to find work (Hublou, CA 1991).

In each type of job, however, there are basic actions that used to analyze the good faith efforts of a job search.

- Frequency and hours of job search efforts

  - How many days per week or month

  - How many hours per day

  - How many hours that coincide with normal work hours of the field

- Consistency of job search efforts

- Number of job search efforts

- Timing of job search efforts

- Methods used in job searches

- Geography of jobs sought

- Appropriateness of job search efforts to the type of job sought

- Job search, resume writing, and Internet use skills

- Interviewing skills

While it is important to put enough time into job search to build knowledge and momentum, the schedule for putting in the time varies by the job seeker's energy and by the work patterns of the jobs he or she is seeking.

Examples of timing of job search activities according to job title and personal choice:

I usually spend two or three hours on Sunday night doing online research so, I'm ready to make calls on Monday.

I'm in construction, so I have to call possible employers by 7 or 8 a.m. They're out in the field after that and they only take dispatcher calls then.

I'm a lawyer so I have to call people after about 4 p.m. Otherwise, they're in court or with clients.

No, you can't call most salons on Mondays. They're closed.

I'm in the hospitality field. I can't get through to anyone during the lunch or dinner hours, but about 2 to 3 p.m. is usually good.

Stockbrokers work on New York hours, so on the West Coast, they're at work by 4 or 5a.m. and gone by 1 or 2 p.m.

Monday mornings are good times to call retailers. No one shops early on Monday, or most days really, unless there's a big sale.

I'm a late night person, so I usually do my research online after 10 p.m. But I wonder if employers notice what time of day I send in applications or emails.

Methods of effective job search can vary by the type of job sought and its rank. The size of the firm also influences the way employers hire, and thus the methods job seekers should use to find positions.

For instance, workers find skilled trade jobs through unions or direct employer contact on a job site. Colleges and universities fill academic jobs through contacts made at conferences held by the professional organization for academic specialties and through their journals. Accounting and administrative jobs can be found through staffing agencies. High-echelon executive jobs are accessible almost exclusively through personal networking contacts and specialized recruiters.

"A sizable fraction (20 percent) of hiring occurs without any recruiting [placing job ads or using staffing or recruiting agencies]. This is some of the most striking evidence in support of the informal channels [personal contacts or networking] . . . as an important recruiting tool." (Faberman, 2011) Employers that hire without a vacancy announcement use informal hiring more in some occupations, less in others. For instance, companies fill clerical and sales jobs through job announcements almost twice as often as management and structural work jobs. Almost 30 percent of the management and structural jobs are filled with no formal recruiting; 22 percent of professional and technical occupations are informal hires.

Generally, larger firms interview more workers and invest more time in recruiting; this tendency rises with the size of the starting salary and with higher or more specialized skills essential to the job.

Helping job seekers understand the most effective ways they can reach employers' notice is an important benefit of the vocational evaluation.

EARNING CAPACITY OF EVALUEES WHO ARE WORKING

Work banishes those three great evils: boredom, vice, and poverty.

Voltaire

The earning capacity for someone who is working is less frequently the subject of a vocational evaluation. Earnings can equal earning capacity, although this equation is not always applicable. The vocational evaluator enters when there is doubt about the reasonableness of the income a working person is earning. Just as a job seeker is judged for good faith efforts to find work, a working person is evaluated to determine if her or his earnings constitute reasonable compensation.

Examples of situations in which actual earnings do not represent earning capacity can vary in both directions, either higher or lower. For instance, a person who is not skilled enough to compete in the open labor market may be paid more generously in a family business or friend's company than she or he could realistically expect in a position without that personal connection. In this instance, the pay would be higher than earning capacity. Or a person can defer receiving compensation from a family business to show lower earnings or to help the business through cash flow problems. A person who is working fewer hours than full time, or not working as much overtime as he or she used to, may have an income lower than expected but not be suppressing income.

In Simpson (CA 1992), the California Supreme Court found that the supporting spouse's choice to trade "an extraordinary work regimen" of many more than 40 hours per week for an "objectively reasonable work regimen" was a valid decision. In the discussion of the Bardzik decision, the court wrote that the purpose of determining earning capacity was not necessarily to find "a per se 'last and highest income' " which would not only be contrary to statute, but unwise and unnecessary as well.

Some people work in jobs in nonprofit settings doing work that would pay significantly more if they were performing the tasks in a for-profit business. In this example, earning capacity may be more than actual income.

A cogent example for judges is the earning capacity of a judge employed by a Superior or district court compared to what that same professional could earn in a private legal practice. Most judges observe that they are opting to do a valuable job that remunerates them less than optimally; they understand that other employed parties can be in similar positions.

For evaluators, the questions occur about whether the working person has available employment alternatives, what those other jobs pay, and whether the person is working as many hours as he or she can. In some professions, the standard hours seem less than full time to outside observers.

For example, in some geographic locations, it is customary for nurses to work 4 eight-hour shifts per week, or 32 hours rather than 40 hours per week. This pattern may have been the subject of union contract or other employer-employee negotiations. Some nurses combine two part time jobs to fill the 40-hour per week capacity, but many acknowledge the strain of the job by working the standard 32 hours per week. The evaluator's task is to determine whether it is reasonable to consider a 32-hour week as full time employment in the designated job.

Similarly, those employees who work in corporations may view teachers as working less than full time, since classes end at 2:00 or 3:00 p.m. and summer vacations last eight weeks or more. They may not be aware of the additional hours teachers typically spend grading papers, developing curriculum, handling administrative tasks, and working with students and their parents outside of classroom time.

It is the evaluator's function to determine how many hours the person is actually working, whether additional work is available, and what the local standards are, so that the person's work efforts and the adequacy of their compensation can be assessed.

EARNING CAPACITY OF EVALUEES IN SELF-EMPLOYMENT

By working faithfully eight hours a day, you may get to be a boss – and work twelve hours a day.

Benjamin Franklin, *Poor Richard's Almanac*

Self-employment is one way to reenter the labor market commonly mentioned when evaluees first express an interest in work. Some evaluees start the vocational evaluation already engaged in self-employment, either part time or full time. If an evaluee is successfully working in a self-employment enterprise, the evaluation process parallels that for anyone who is working for an employer.

For those who are not yet started or well established in their own business, many aspects of self-employment — some real, some imagined — encourage the idea of working for oneself. Self-employment often seems like a way to ease into work and to have control over the day's schedule. It commonly feels like the best option for someone who is coordinating a working life with parental responsibilities. It may appear less daunting than facing the multiple rejections from employers that job seekers expect after being away from the work force for years.

The structure of spousal support often is based on a projected period for the evaluee to find work and earn a predictable income. If poorly planned self-employment falls through and generates only a fraction of the anticipated income, the supported spouse may have difficulty requesting extended spousal support to cover the period until employment income begins. Unprofitability will create an added support burden in divorces, where predictable income production is legally expected. It is the evaluator's responsibility to assess self-employment ideas for viability as a vocational option, and its ability to produce a consistent income stream.

During the recession of 2008-2011, when job search durations doubled, the time for small businesses to reach profitability began to look less daunting in comparison. In times of lower unemployment rates, when a job hunter could find work in three to six months but a new small business could take a year to become profitable, employment was preferable to self-employment. In the economic climate in which it could take a job seeker, especially one with an extended absence from the labor market, six to twelve months to find work, a well-designed self-employment plan might have an equal chance of producing a profit within a similar period to a job hunt.

The vocational evaluator can help a would-be entrepreneur avoid delays in income production and the distress of a failure in business by understanding common causes of failure to analyze the proposed business. If the business is complex, out of the evaluator's area of expertise, or advanced, a skilled small business planner can use these criteria to assess the likelihood of success. Business planners are listed with the U.S. Small Business Association, its SCORE (Service Corps of Retired Executives) program or local business incubator programs.

ASSESSING SELF-EMPLOYMENT PROPOSALS FOR VIABILITY

It is essential not to reject even poorly developed proposals for self-employment when evaluees bring them up in the interview. An experienced evaluator may make a quick judgment that the idea is not viable or sounds unlikely to succeed. Saying so immediately does not afford evaluees the time and information to think about the project that they would have in a guided conversation. The final decision about proceeding or abandoning the self-employment idea is the evaluees', not the evaluator's.

An evaluator's quick laugh, "*Oh, that'll never work. Let's think about a job you can find*" is disrespectful and can result in the evaluee's lack of cooperation with a subsequent plan, even one that is more realistic. The evaluee may say, after sessions in vocational planning, "*You never listened to my idea and I still think it would work. I'm not going to work for someone else till I get a chance to work at my dream of self-employment.*"

Self-employment is not easier than working for an employer. It is important to lead the evaluee through the necessary thinking about self-employment and give him or her assignments to complete to investigate the viability of the idea.

For every business, planning, setting goals, and creating metrics or measures of future success against which to measure actual performance are essential. An evaluee who is not deeply invested enough in his or her self-employment plan to do major research into normal business intelligence, such as the competition, startup and ongoing overhead costs, financial details, and marketing methods, is demonstrating a lack of commitment to the plan that is predictive of its failure. Each person who wants to be self-employed should be both willing and able to think in detail about what will make the business successful.

Mary, a highly skilled woman who made excellent fruitcakes and Christmas decorations, sold them successfully through the people in her husband's company every December. She was a real craftsperson with new ideas and loved to work with her hands. Her self-employment idea was to open a small shop in a local strip mall near her house and expand her craft items beyond the Christmas season to make decorative household items to sell all year round. I asked her to talk to the strip mall management to get an idea of store rental costs and we set a second appointment.

When Mary returned, we talked through her shop idea. Rents, she had found, would be about $1000 per month. To get a rough estimate of her expenses, we added in other basic monthly costs: phone and computer connections, utilities, and startup costs such as display counters, business software, inventory and craft supplies, marketing collateral, and some basic advertising. Then I asked her about the details of the items she was planning to sell. Christmas ornaments usually sold between $3 and $20 each. Without worrying yet about the cost of the supplies, we figured out how many items she would have to sell each month just to meet expenses. If her expenses were $2500 per month with no employees, and her average item sold for $10, she would have to sell 250 every month before she made a profit. This did not take into account many other aspects of the business; we just wanted to start with the basics. I asked her how long it took her to make each ornament; she figured it was about 30-45 minutes each, so 250 items would take her no less than 125 hours, or three weeks in the month. She was startled at the realization that she would be spending three full weeks doing handwork, in addition to running a business, and recognized that much production would be tedious and repetitive, hard on her hands and eyes and back, and didn't sound like *much fun. Mary decided to keep her handwork as a hobby. She felt satisfied that we had paid enough attention to her idea to take it, and her skills, seriously, and that the decision not to proceed was hers. She then was ready to move on to thinking about employment.*

Denise had more than half time custody of her children, six and eight, and their semi-rural location made it essential that she be able to take the kids to school and pick them up daily. Flexibility was the main criterion for her career choice. She was not strongly interested in finishing a degree. A young and healthy woman who loved to be outdoors with her own pets, she proposed a dog walking and pet sitting service as her employment plan. She had already called several people who provided similar services in her area to find out what they charged and how they marketed their services.

With guidance, she worked out a schedule to spend 25 hours per week for the next several weeks investigating how viable her idea was. She committed to doing more information gathering, writing a marketing plan, and listing her probable expenses and likely revenue. We pointed her toward the web sites and local chapters of professional organizations of dog walkers and pet sitters so that she could see the situations they had confronted and solved: contracts, being paid, cancellations, rates to charge for differing services, insurance, covering illnesses and vacations, interactions with difficult pet owners, deciding on a geographic area to serve, and more. We also brainstormed ways she could market her services to get started: a flyer or brochure at every vet's office and pet food store, coffee shop and grocery in her chosen locale; conversations with neighbors and friends; and a basic website. We discussed marketing collateral, agreeing she should not spend much at first on a logo design or business cards, and setting her up to take a few classes at the closest Small Business Association to learn about bookkeeping and taxes.

By the time of Denise's third vocational appointment, we were able to draw up a plan that would allow her to earn at least as much in self-employment as she could have earned working for someone else. She was delighted with the structured support she had received and was much more confident in launching her business. Because the steps were clear, the attorneys were comfortable that she could be held accountable. Her potential income was projected for the next 6 to 12 months with a possible review if problems arose, so support was based on those figures. Her business became profitable soon after she started.

The assignments for an evaluee to explain why a self-employment idea is a preferred vocational option should help a would-be entrepreneur plan for success; they are not make-work or distractions from the real work of being in business. New entrepreneurs often feel that planning is a digression from the tasks they see as directly related to building the business, although planning proves very helpful to ensuring success. Lack of follow through on these assignments can be a strong indicator to the evaluator that the evaluee is not ready to be self-employed. The willingness of the evaluee to take the serious steps to attend classes, to expose his ideas to assessment and modification, and to spend time on planning is an excellent indicator of the depth of his capacity to build a self-employment plan that will create an income that will match the effort involved.

Describing lack of follow through on assignments is not a method to blame the evaluee. Pointing it out without rancor or shaming can help the evaluee recognize just how much work self-employment will be. These are behavioral signs under the control of the evaluee, not subjective impressions of the evaluator. The behavior is demonstrating both to the evaluator and to the would-be business owner that he or she does not want to do the kind of work needed to create a viable enterprise. This self-awareness can lead the evaluee to a willing decision to set aside self-employment as a full time earnings option, and allows the evaluee to move to the next decisions.

An evaluee can learn to judge his or her self-employment idea by attending Small Business Administration classes, speaking to a representative from the Service Corps of Retired Executive (SCORE, a project of the SBA), or attending classes at programs aimed at helping new entrepreneurs, often called business incubators. In San Francisco, the business incubator called the Renaissance Entrepreneurship Center offers a wide variety of classes, both preliminary assessments of self-employment dreams and more detailed training to develop a clear business plan. Newcomers to self-employment can investigate their potential for success by discussing their ideas with self-employed entrepreneurs already functioning successfully.

The National Business Incubator Association (NBIA, www.nbia.org) lists national and international incubation programs and state associations in Alabama, Arkansas, Colorado, Connecticut, Florida, Indiana, Louisiana, Maryland, Massachusetts, Michigan, Mississippi, Missouri, New Hampshire, New York, North Carolina, Oklahoma, Pennsylvania, Texas, Virginia, Washington, and Wisconsin.

ANALYZING SELF-EMPLOYMENT FOR EARNING CAPACITY

One challenge for vocational evaluators is to determine a self-employed person's earning capacity. One measure, of course, is actual net earnings — net profits after expenses are deducted from revenues. Problems with using this single figure are the many incentives and opportunities the self-employed have to make this number as low as possible. The lower the profit, the less they pay in taxes and the less they may have as attributed income either to pay or to receive spousal or child support.

To determine what a self-employed person can be earning, an evaluator can a) look at actual earnings, b) compare the actual self-employed earnings to those of others in their situations as self-employed persons, or c) compare the self-employed earnings to those of people performing similar work while employed.

A spousal support case, Iredale vs. Cates (CA 2004), addresses earning capacity in those cases where the individual is in a professional occupation or self-employed. (Tracy and Wallace, 2010) The court found that the "average salaried person" standard is not the only valid measure for establishing reasonable compensation for a self-employed professional (in this case, an attorney). Substantial evidence of the standard earnings of "similarly situated professionals" can also indicate earning capacity.

> *Joe, a carpenter who does framing and general residential repair work, has been self-employed for a decade but is earning much less now than in past years. Joe says that the reason for the decrease is that the construction market has declined. He reports that activity in house repair has dipped because of general market conditions and his smaller income reflects the decrease in demand that many others in his field are experiencing.*

To decide whether his current income represents his full earning capacity, the evaluator compares Joe's experience to other carpenter-handymen's experiences, researches the general market conditions, and speaks to other self-employed carpenters.

The evaluator will ask questions involving the self-employed carpenter's hourly rates, ability to estimate projects accurately, skills in performing the projects he contracts to do. Some of the most important questions are how he markets his work and targets his potential customers, and how much time he spends on getting new jobs and making new contacts.

For the carpenter-handyman, the evaluator can call other self-employed carpenters and ask about the market, earning ranges, and hourly rates, how earnings are doing this year compared to prior years, how much time the carpenters spend in finding new business, and how many projects they do weekly or monthly. This can help the evaluator determine whether the decrease in income is a widespread phenomenon or only the individual's experience. The evaluator can also speak to contractors who hire carpenters about their perceptions of the availability of work, standard expectations of hours and wages, benefits, and time off.

Skilled workers in self-employment often charge hourly rates that seem high, but these amounts also compensate for the unpaid time they spend on business tasks. A carpenter not only spends time repairing the house he is working on, he drives to and from the project, plans the materials, goes to pick the materials up and unloads them, removes old materials and disposes of them, cares for his tools, spends time on the phone speaking to the customer, clarifying the assignment and its progress. Hourly rates higher than employed carpenters receive also help the independent carpenter manage time when he has no work. Part of the evaluator's task is to determine how many billable hours are reasonable for a self-employed person annually. This is rarely as many as the 2,080 hours used to calculate yearly income for employed people who are paid an hourly wage for 52 weeks, 40 hours per week as a full time employee.

Lack of skill or knowledge is not the most common reason self-employment fails. Some new entrepreneurs are unrealistic about how much work it takes to find potential customers (marketing) and to complete the deal to get the assignment (sales). Questions about marketing and sales activities can test whether the carpenter is spending as much time as his or her peers in doing the necessary business aspects of the job.

Another way to estimate earning capacity for someone earning less than expected in self-employment is to investigate what income those same skills would bring an employed person. After all, if a person is doing all the tasks of self-employment and not earning as much as he could if he were working for someone else, he should be looking very carefully at the alternative of closing the less lucrative business and finding a job. These decisions may apply to people who are self-employed but perhaps should not be.

If they choose not to shift from self-employment to working for an employer, and employment is a real option in the labor market, this choice to earn less can lead to an imputed income higher than the actual earnings. The assumption in family law is that a person will create the best earnings of which they are capable as quickly as possible toward their self-support. The trier of fact in family law cases does not have to use the maximum a person can earn as the earning capacity, as seen in the California decisions in Everett (1990), Padilla (1995), and Simpson (1992) cases, but the earner should be trying to do his or her best to create income.

In the commentary in the Bardzik case, the court quotes from Everett, stating that:

the court said in a remarkably sensitive passage: The trial court's task is more delicate than simply deciding that because a parent might be able to earn more money, additional income should be imputed to that parent . . . . [¶] . . . . Maybe the restructuring would not work out and the parent's financial situation and mental well-being would deteriorate. All of these factors are interrelated; while ultimately the court must consider earning capacity to the extent consistent with the best interests of the children, their best interest of course is affected by the economic as well as emotional strength of the supporting parent.

The evaluator's responsibility in these situations is to state for the parties and triers of fact the potential earnings of an employed person performing the same job as the self-employed evaluee, and account for the differences in earnings. The vocational expert should form conclusions, if possible, about whether the potential self-employment plan is viable and whether to recommend it. A negative opinion should explain why the evaluator does not expect the plan to be successful in comparison to employment alternatives.

SELF-EMPLOYMENT FOR STABLE INCOME PRODUCTION

The concern about self-employment in family law cases is that the income produced will not be large enough or consistent enough to be predictable. The supporting spouse wants to minimize the support amount and eliminate the prospect of making up for a business's failure; the supported spouse wants to create certainty in managing household expenses. Whether the self-employed person is the source or recipient of support, the uncertainty of self-employment compensation and the suspicion of mixed motivations to report income accurately make predicting a stable income from self-employment problematic.

About one in nine workers (10.9 percent of the total employed) was self-employed in 2009; as in the past, self-employment continues to be more common among men, Whites and Asians, and older workers, and the more educated. Self-employment is higher in the construction industry and in business services and for management, scientific, and technical consulting services. (Hipple, 2010)

Small businesses often fail. Of 100 businesses started, 36 percent have failed by the second year and 50 percent of them have failed by the fourth year. Over the course of ten years, only 29 percent of businesses are still functioning. (Shane, 2008)

The Small Business Association lists the ten most common causes for small businesses to fail or to close: 1) lack of experience, 2) insufficient capital, 3) poor location, 4) poor inventory management, 5) over-investment in fixed assets, 6) poor credit arrangements, 7) personal use of business funds, 8) unexpected growth, 9) competition, and 10) low sales. (Ames, 1983) Another analysis adds further reasons for small business failure: lack of adequate cash flow, poor business planning, unworkable goals, poor system of control, and lack of entrepreneurial skills. (Titus, 2003)

Many people attempt self-employment quickly without doing much preliminary business planning. That approach sometimes works, especially in situations where a backup income from a spouse exists in case of failure. Starting a business quickly utilizes the initial enthusiasm but may prolong the period before the business becomes profitable, or even lead to failure. Serial entrepreneurship in businesses that function for a while but do not progress or grow is a common pattern. Also common are part-time small businesses that cannot grow large enough to cover a household's entire budget needs reliably.

The vocational evaluator can help direct some of the preliminary planning for self-employment as part of the assessment of the plan's likelihood of success, but does not function as the major source of business advice. The business plan should stand up to scrutiny, to see if the projected revenues are achievable, the expenses proportional, the evaluee's skills sufficient, and the market likely to be open enough to the new service or product for a foreseeable profit.

In the Berger case (CA 2009), the husband opened a landscaping company that was not producing sufficient income. He opted not to take a salary, thereby investing profits that would have supported him back into the company. The Berger court held that his voluntary choice to do without income did not change his obligation to support his children.

In Shaughnessy (CA 2006), the wife was told that her floral business that netted only $650 per month was "not the means for her continued long term economic well being".

FREQUENT TYPES OF SELF-EMPLOYMENT PROPOSALS

Many self-employment proposals heard in vocational evaluations resemble these descriptions.

- People who are already working part time in small home-based sales structures. They may be a part of a larger organization with a multi-level marketing (MLM) structure, in which the person both sells products and recruits others. The recruits sell under her auspices and she receives a percentage of their sales. The products might be a cosmetic line, home wares, clothing, or nutriceuticals (personal care and other products to enhance appearance and health). Alternatively, they might be doing direct consumer sales through home parties.

  I've been selling high-end clothes in trunk shows for years. My friends love it. I recruit new people and I get a percentage of their commissions. I make about $40,000 a year. No, that's before I deduct expenses. I don't really work out how much my expenses are. I get great clothes though. It's hard to tell how much I'm going to earn because it depends on how much the people below me are selling. I don't get those numbers. I depend on the company to figure all that out. I'm not great at bookkeeping, to tell you the truth. I just love selling clothes

- People who work in an arts endeavor – music, painting, writing, graphics, film – who now are seeking to expand the work to full time and want to create a livable income from their work.

  I'm a musician. That's all I've ever done and I have a degree in it. I have five CDs and I perform with my group and two others. We get a lot of gigs and I just have to get more. I could make better money if I got a chance to compose for film.

- People working as freelance consultants, as in computers or business areas, often utilizing the skills developed in large corporations they have left either by layoff or by termination. Their clients may continue to work with them as an extension of a relationship initially built while they were employed in the enterprise.

  I'm a marketing consultant. I used to work for a big marketing group but I was laid off two years ago. I got some great assignments from old clients for a while. Now those contacts have moved to other companies and I'm not getting as much work these days.

- People who offer a service such as accounting or bookkeeping, medical or legal transcription, tutoring, or college teaching, as independent contractors for several stable clients.

I do bookkeeping for three sole proprietors, not every week, but I've done it for years now. It pays okay and it's very flexible. Not my favorite thing to do, but it works in my life right now.

- People who create a craft product – jewelry, specialty foods, clothing, decorative items – and sell them sporadically throughout the year, who envision scaling their work up to a stable retail location.

I'm a great baker and I'm known for my cupcakes and kids' birthday cakes. I sell them to the people at my husband's work. Well, that's not going to happen anymore, I guess. I knit kids' sweaters too and I bet I could sell them at craft fairs or even open a little shop in the mall near me and teach people how to scrapbook, and crochet and knit. I do all those things.

- People who perform project-based work such as construction, repair, or transportation, as independent contractors who find work through word of mouth, unions, or from a base of several businesses.

I'm a handyman. I can fix anything around the house, you name it. Locks, faucets, toilets, windows and doors. I paint, I lay floors, I do some carpentry, I've even worked with concrete. I can do it all.

- People who are entering a new occupation in which most practitioners are independent contractors or combine part-time employment with independent practices, such as psychotherapists and other counselors, massage therapists or yoga instructors, real estate agents, or hairdressers, manicurists, and estheticians.

I'm working on getting my 3,000 supervised hours doing psychotherapy so I can take the MFT (Marriage and Family Therapist) exam. I've been talking to some of the people in my sons' schools about getting referrals because I want to work mostly with families. I don't have a marketing plan. I just talk to people about what I'm doing.

- People who have been working in a family business in which they cannot continue after the divorce because of the ruptured relationship. For these employees, who may have had a financial ownership position or an emotional connection as an owner, the challenge may be finding a new job with the same flexibility, accommodation for personal and family hours, and acceptance of their skills.

I work in the family business doing the receivables and payables. About 20 hours a week. Well, I used to. It's a really old program; my mother-in-law set it up and she taught me how to use it. No, I don't use QuickBooks.

- People with executive corporate experience whose financial successes have allowed them to retire early, with ideas of their next steps focusing on creating a startup business.

I already know what I want to do and I have enough money to do it. I'm starting a new company, we call it NewCo, and it will take a couple years to get off the ground.

- And most recently, those who create web sites and use social media for marketing with the hope that attracting advertisers and viewers will bring in a consistent income.

EARNING CAPACITY FOR EVALUEES IN FAMILY-OWNED BUSINESSES

A common scenario in evaluating earning capacity and work skills arises when the evaluee has been working in a family-owned business. Evaluees sometimes describe this as being self-employed, sometimes as employed. Some of the evaluees working for a family company grew up in the business, learned the job and the industry well, and developed an extended base of knowledge that he or she can transfer to another job.

Example A) The family business is plumbing and the evaluee's job is estimating the costs of a particular project to create the bid the plumber submits to the contractor. The estimator probably has many skills that will be useful in other settings: knowledge of plumbing methods and how long the projects take, supplies and vendors, labor costs and availability, and which supplies and tools are essential to particular types of projects. The estimator probably also has customer service skills, math skills, and sales ability. If the job in the family business becomes unavailable, other occupations and positions are open to the estimator.

If, however, the person working in the self-employment enterprise within the family is doing only a portion of the job that most employers expect, the skills will not transfer as easily.

Example B) A spouse marries into a family with an established business. She stays at home raising the children until the business gets busier and they want an extra hand in the office. The job is not well defined and she willingly fills in where there are tasks to be done. The spouse helps out in the business part time, sending out invoices and entering bookkeeping data, coordinating the work schedules of the contractors, and maybe talking to customers occasionally, balancing these tasks with the demands of child care and housekeeping. She keeps a stable but somewhat irregular schedule that increases in hours during busy times, then decreases when the kids are sick or the family takes a vacation. Now that the couple is divorcing, the spouse will not continue working in the family business and has to consider finding new work.

The vocational evaluation will assess the transferability of the work skills the spouse gained in the family business office. It may be that this small business established its office practices long ago and has not kept up with new business methods, so the bookkeeping and accounting may be simpler than in most businesses, idiosyncratic in its forms and records, or not up-to-date in the software it uses.

A job title arbitrarily bestowed in a family business may – or may not – reflect the skills required by mainstream employers of workers with the same title. Someone who has no management responsibilities may carry the title of Manager, so a new employer will not hire her as a manager or see her as sufficiently experienced to handle those tasks. Even with the title Office Manager, this worker may not be qualified to work in a slightly larger office that uses different software, standard business forms, or newer office machines. Larger businesses may expect their office managers to do many more tasks than this part-time worker in the family business, tasks that could include training, hiring, human resources and benefits management, and handling several staff who report directly to her.

Jobs in a family owned business may not fully prepare a worker to transfer to an outside employer. Family businesses readily make accommodations or adjustments to work around an employee's lack of skills or interests. If someone is not good at filing or math, someone else who does those tasks better or likes them more will perform them. If they do not like talking to strangers, they may not be required to work at the service counter. Supervisors may tolerate and correct repeated mistakes that family employees make. However, in non-family businesses, these tasks may be standard parts of the job description and excuses or mistakes are not acceptable. The job that is hand-built around a person's abilities and preferences may not give them sufficient transferable skills or allow them to perform the job tasks that are customary in the open labor market.

Workers in family businesses may have real skills but perhaps have no experience in selling their services or creating a set of credentials that can get them hired by nonfamily customers.

Example C) Giselle and her husband Donovan, a dentist, are divorcing.

> *Donovan tells the evaluator about Giselle's skills in interior decoration. "She's terrific. You should see our house; she did it all and worked with the contractor and it looks great. She has really good taste. When I opened my new office, she came in and decided on the chairs and tables, the wall colors in the treatment rooms and the waiting room. She even talked to the contractor about layout. I'm sure she can work as an interior decorator."*

The evaluator will determine whether Giselle's skilled but amateur work will qualify her for hire as an interior design professional with no further training or experience. Because of her role as wife, she may have avoided some of the essential, non-design tasks that interior designers often undertake. She never, for instance, had to sell her ideas to a client, work with a client's own taste and style preferences rather than her own, or be constrained by a budget over which she had no control. She may not know important building codes or design software. Learning about the realities of actual employer demands may modify her husband's expectations that she is immediately employable and can earn the average salary for an interior designer.

Prior earnings may not be the best basis of estimates of future earnings for evaluees who have been working in family businesses. In a family business, compensation is often set for reasons unrelated to standard pay for the job the evaluee is doing. To avoid taxes or to manage a time of poor cash flow, family businesses may pay the evaluee below market value. Alternatively, to bring income into the family, the family business may pay a family member who is working part time at a much higher hourly rate than she or he could get in the open market. These pay ranges may not vary to reflect competence or incompetence on the job, so earnings within the family business may not create realistic compensation expectations for work in the open labor market.

◆ ◆ ◆

In assessing earning capacity, the questions and focus change with the work status of the evaluee, but all point to a single aim for the conclusions: to describe the evaluee's potential income and position in relation to the world of work.

It is of the nature of man, when he is not diseased, to take pleasure in his work . . . .

William Morris in *Useful Work vs Useless Toil* (1885)

Through the methodology of the structured interview and testing, the evaluator analyzes ability to work, one major element of the definition of earning capacity. As part of that, the evaluator learns about the evaluee's physical and mental capacities. If necessary, the evaluator considers the influence of a health condition on ability to work – either the health of the evaluee, or the health or special needs of the dependent children.

Health is one of the standard areas of focus in nonforensic vocational assessment and vocational counseling, and the California Family Code lists the topic as a factor for consideration. The factors related to the ability to work mandated for consideration in the California Family Code are:

- Age
- Health
- Education
- Marketable skills
- Employment history

Of the fifty states and the District of Columbia, forty states' statutes specifically mention health as a factor to be considered in setting spousal support. Of the remainder, several states' statutes include general factors that could include health as determinant of support, using terminology such as "the unique circumstances," "the circumstances of the parties," "the respective merits of the spouses," or "the character and situation of the parties." (Tracy & Wallace, 2008)

State	Statutory language concerning health as a factor to be considered in establishing spousal support
Alabama	— Not stated
Alaska	The age and health of the parties
Arizona	The physical and emotional condition of the spouses
Arkansas	—Not stated; general: parties' earning ability and capacity
California	The age and health of the spouses
Colorado	The age and the health condition of the spouse seeking maintenance
Connecticut	The health of the parties
Delaware	The age, and health condition of both parties
District of Columbia	— Not stated
Florida	The age and health of each party

State	Statutory language concerning health as a factor to be considered in establishing spousal support
Georgia	The age and medical condition of each party
Hawaii	Health condition of the parties
Idaho	The age and the physical and emotional condition of the party seeking maintenance
Illinois	The age and health condition of both parties
Indiana	If the court finds a spouse to be physically or mentally incapacitated to the extent that the ability of the incapacitated spouse to support himself or herself is materially affected, the court may find that maintenance for the spouse is necessary during the period of incapacity, subject to further order of the court
Iowa	The age and health of the parties
Kansas	— Not stated
Kentucky	The age and health condition of the parties
Louisiana	The health and age of the parties
Maine	The health and disabilities of each party
Maryland	The health conditions of the spouses
Massachusetts	Health
Michigan	— Not stated. General: character and situation of the parties
Minnesota	The age and health condition of the spouse who desires maintenance
Mississippi	The spouse's health and medical condition
Missouri	The age and health condition of the spouse seeking maintenance
Montana	The age and the health condition of the spouse seeking maintenance
Nebraska	— Not stated. General: the circumstances of the parties
Nevada	— Not stated. General: The respective merits of the spouses
New Hampshire	Health condition
New Jersey	The age and health condition of each of the parties
New Mexico	The age and medical condition of each spouse
New York	The length of the marriage and the age and health of the parties
North Carolina	The ages and the health conditions of the spouses
North Dakota	— Not stated. General: the unique circumstances of the parties
Ohio	The ages and the health conditions of the parties
Oklahoma	— Not stated
Oregon	The health condition of the parties
Pennsylvania	The ages and health condition of the parties
Rhode Island	The health condition, age, station, occupation, amount and source of income, job skills, and employability of the parties
South Carolina	The health condition of each spouse
South Dakota	The health condition of the spouses
Tennessee	The health condition of the spouse
Texas	The age, employment history, earning ability, and health condition of the spouse seeking maintenance
Utah	— Not stated

State	Statutory language concerning health as a factor to be considered in establishing spousal support
Vermont	The age and health condition of each spouse
Virginia	The age and health condition of the parties and any special circumstances of the family
Washington	The age and health condition, and financial obligations of the spouse seeking maintenance
West Virginia	The ages and the health condition of each party
Wisconsin	The age and health of the parties
Wyoming	— Not stated

ABILITY TO WORK – HEALTH AND DISABILITY

HEALTH OF THE EVALUEE

The health of the spouse, especially in long-term marriages with an older spouse, can arise as a major barrier to employment and thus become a consideration in determining earning capacity. Physical constraints can limit an employee's work hours, types of jobs, commute distance, and consistent attendance at work. Mental incapability can affect concentration, learning speed, complexity of possible job tasks, and the ability to interview or maintain work relationships.

The first awareness that an individual's health could be an important topic can come from several sources. The referring attorney in the initial call to the evaluator may say,

I think the person you'll be seeing is going to talk about trouble working. I've seen signs of depression. We haven't really talked much about it, but it could come up.

The evaluee may report a health problem openly to the evaluator.

I can't work. I have severe IBS [irritable bowel syndrome] and fibromyalgia. It's bad more than a couple of days a week and I can't even leave the house about three or four days a month. I never know when it's going to hit me, and I always have to be close to a bathroom. I feel achy all over, that's the fibromyalgia, and some days I can't even get out of bed.

The evaluee may mention his or her medical history as part of a thorough vocational interview.

I had breast cancer five years ago but I'm done with radiation and chemo. Except for my checkups, it won't affect my work. I'm okay.

I have a bad back and I can't lift too much. It's usually okay, but I have to be careful. I'm a physical therapist but I haven't worked in about seven years. I want to go back because that's where I'll be paid best, but if I'm working with stroke patients, it'll be too much lifting. I just have to figure out if there are PT jobs, like in a hand clinic, where I don't have to lift patients.

Sometimes the evaluator identifies the evaluee's disability, spotting signs of disability-related dysfunction that have been ignored, by listening to the evaluee's daily activities and where problems occur. This is especially true of significant mental or psychological conditions, but can also happen for physical problems.

I was working with an evaluee I had seen once before, a woman about 55 with a professional background. She had lost a long-term job and we were discussing her future job options. She sat across the desk from me, propping her elbow on the edge of the desk, with her head in her hand, her fingers covering her eyes. Although she was talking freely, she wasn't looking at me.

"Sylvia, are you mad at me? Or depressed?" I asked her finally, a little exasperated that she wouldn't make eye contact. She had done this in the first meeting, too, but I had attributed it to reluctance to participate in the evaluation. But she wasn't sounding or acting reluctant today. "Do you have a headache?"

She dropped her hand, angled her head far back on her neck, and peered at me from under her eyelids. "No," she said, puzzled. "I'm not mad at you. I'm fine. Why?"

"You're not looking at me. You're holding your head in your hand and you're looking down at the desk."

"Oh," she said, "I can't. My eyelids droop so far down that I need to lift them up with my fingers or I can't see. And if I don't, I get a stiff neck from leaning so far back." She explained that she had ptosis, eyelid drooping caused by weakness of the muscle responsible for raising the eyelid, damage to the nerves that control those muscles, or looseness of the skin of the upper eyelids.

"Have you seen the doctor?" I asked. "Of course," she replied, "but he said that I'd need surgery to correct it and the insurance won't pay for it because they think of it as cosmetic surgery."

We talked more about her ptosis problem and Sylvia realized that if she needed to use one hand to prop up her eyelids, not only would she have difficulty using a computer keyboard, she'd have a hard time getting through an employment interview successfully. She was even driving one-handed. She was so used to it, she hadn't realized how the ptosis made her appear to others —uninterested or disengaged. Everyone at her old job had just accepted that Sylvia looked like that; a new employer might not be so understanding.

Emboldened by the letter I wrote for her insurance company explaining that Sylvia's eyelid droop was causing work problems for her and was not just a cosmetic concern, Sylvia saw her doctor again. After her insurance company agreed to pay for her blepharoplasty (repair of droopy eyelids), Sylvia came back in with eyes wide open, smiling and looking 10 years younger. We happily continued her vocational planning, and this time we could both look at each other.

Much dysfunction can be veiled within a marriage. Many marital partners fill in for the incompetence of the spouse, earning the income, paying the bills, making the decisions, structuring the family life. The functional partner may not see the lack of ability to perform these functions in the spouse. Some partners do not extrapolate their experiences with the spouse to understand that employers will also find the behaviors problematic. These same dysfunctional patterns could indicate a mental health problem that may interfere with finding or keeping work.

The competent partner may interpret the spouse's lack of daily functioning as voluntary – laziness, passive aggression, lack of caring or love – or involuntary – being "scattered," lacking organization skills, or having a silly personality quirk that used to be endearing and now is annoying.

Can never find the way, gets lost all the time.

Always late, can't get anywhere on time.

Has moods and doesn't always get meals made or even get out of bed. Doesn't get the kids ready for school half the time or make their lunches.

Doesn't do much except clean and shop.

Can't plan or manage anything; the house is always a mess and all the bills were paid late till I started doing them.

Can't finish a project. Always jumps from one idea to another without thinking it through.

Can't get along with anybody. Has been fired so many times I can't even count them.

These behaviors may be not be signs of disability but of boredom or lack of interest, distraction, situational depression that lifts, or anger; or they may be signs of significant emotional problems such as bipolar disorder, severe attention deficit hyperactivity disorder (ADHD), or other diagnoses that are to be taken into account when determining ability to work or creating a reentry plan.

DISTINGUISHING BETWEEN IMPAIRMENT AND DISABILITY

The distinction between a diagnosis and its impact on work appears in the use of two different terms:

Impairment is a loss of or abnormality in body structure or physiological function (including mental functions). Abnormality here is used strictly to refer to a significant variation from established statistical norms (i.e., as a deviation from a population mean within measured standard norms) and should be used only this sense (World Health Organization, 2001). A physician or other medical professional most often diagnoses impairment.

Disability describes the barrier to functioning at work or in other situations caused by the impairment. Not all impairments cause work disabilities. Disability is an umbrella term for impairments, activity limitations and participation restrictions. It denotes the negative aspects of the interaction between an individual (with a health condition) and that individual's contextual factors (environmental and personal factors) (World Health Organization, 2001). Not all impairments result in a work disability. The term disability reflects the interplay between the demands of the job and the ability of the person with the impairment, so that impairment may cause a disability in some occupations but not in others. Vocational experts can perform the analysis of job requirements and compare them with the person's functional capacity to form an opinion on the existence of a disability.

For instance, for a person who uses a wheelchair and does not walk, the term impairment describes the diagnosis and the functional difficulties of his or her everyday life. The person who uses a wheelchair may be physically able to work as an attorney, teacher, or financial adviser and may not have a work disability in those occupations; that same person could not work as a welder, truck driver, or carpenter and would have a disability if those occupations with more physical demands were under consideration.

As another example, a diagnosis of diabetes can require time and attention to manage due to the impairment in the body functions. For most people with the diagnosis, diabetes does not interfere with work and does not constitute a disability. For others who lack the ability to manage the disease and its severity, the impairment causes inability to work, a disability. (Havranek, Field, & Grimes, 2005)

A particular diagnosis does not always cause a disability; the disability derives from the interaction of the abilities of the person with the impairment and the demands of the particular occupation or job.

Once there is notice of a medical or psychological problem, the vocational evaluator determines first whether impairment exists and then whether the impairment rises to the status of work disability in relation to the jobs the evaluee might do.

The vocational expert, even one with years of training and experience in working with people with medical or psychological problems, does not make the diagnosis or mandate the actual or prophylactic activity restrictions. The description of the impairment is the expertise of a physician, the treating doctor, or an independent medical examiner.

The expert vocational evaluator's responsibility is to understand the nexus between the evaluee's functional restrictions and capacities and the demands of appropriate jobs to determine the likelihood of the evaluee's getting employment or earning income. Because disability is not a broad concept, but is linked to the demands of particular jobs or occupations that fit the evaluee, primary tasks for the evaluator are to identify those jobs and their physical demands and to compare the demands to the evaluee's physical or mental capacities.

Example A) Essential tremor, in which a person shakes, is noticed mostly in the hands, but may affect the arms, head, and eyelids, especially when the person is trying to control the hands or is under pressure. It is an inconvenient though mostly minor impairment for most people with this diagnosis. Essential tremor becomes a career changer when it is the diagnosis for a law enforcement officer who is required to carry and use a gun, or in a food server who carries trays of beverages. Disability is job-specific.

Example B) An evaluee has been in a car accident and has residual symptoms of back and neck pain. The evaluee's background is in accounting, an occupation that requires long periods of sitting, computer use, keyboarding, looking at a monitor, and attention to detail. Lifting or carrying, bending, walking, and stooping are not significant parts of the accountant job. The evaluee's back pain necessitates frequent shifts in position from sitting to standing and back to sitting. The neck pains preclude looking down for hours at a time and sometimes radiate into the arm. The evaluator's job is to determine whether accounting jobs exist that can accommodate the frequency in position shifts the evaluee needs to stay comfortable and functional at work, and productive enough to meet the employer's demands.

This expert vocational information and the conclusions, along with the medical or psychological reports on which they are based, are conveyed to the trier of fact who can accept or reject the reasoning behind the expert's conclusions, and make the final determination.

ADDRESSING THE ISSUE OF DISABILITY

If the evaluator learns about a disability that could be a barrier to employment, no matter who brings it to light, the evaluator should explore the issue. Ignoring the issue is not an ethical response.

If the medical or psychological problem is at all complex, soliciting applicable professional expertise is the first step. The doctor or therapist describes the impairment and its likely impact on the evaluee's time and physical or mental ability to work. It is the judge, commissioner, or other trier of fact who makes this decision. The vocational evaluator's responsibility is to report to the trier of fact all the information the judge will need to make the decision, especially reports from medical professionals. The vocational evaluator does not exclude relevant but inconvenient or unwelcome information from the report. The vocational evaluator is not the final determiner of the effect of disability on earning capacity, although she or he may bring considerable expertise to the topic.

> The vocational evaluator's responsibility is to provide the trier of fact with all the information the judge will need to make the decision.
>
> A jointly retained vocational expert does not exclude relevant but inconvenient or unwelcome information from the report, even if requested to do so by a referring party or an attorney.

GATHERING HEALTH INFORMATION

The evaluator listens to the evaluees' accounts of their health and daily activities. If they state that they cannot work, the evaluator prepares a form to ask the physicians the questions listed below. The evaluator can also be the person who opens the question of whether the evaluee's functioning will allow her or him to work. The evaluee may be very worried that employers will not accommodate less than perfect health, or not have thought yet about how she will manage her health at work.

If medical information is coming from the treating physician, the evaluator can send the form directly to the physician. It frequently speeds the doctor's response if the evaluee shares the assignment of getting the completed medical form returned with the physician's information and signature. The evaluee also signs a release of information form to allow the physician to reveal confidential medical information. Evaluees have a significant responsibility to assist in collecting medical information to substantiate the existence of a disability, both because the disability affects their work life and because their relationship with the physician makes it more probable that the medical professional will return the form on a timely basis.

Several physician specialists may submit information. For instance, for a person with back pain, neck and arm pain, and depression, medical input may come from an orthopedic surgeon, a neurologist, a pain management specialist, and a psychologist or psychiatrist.

If he has not had recent medical care, an evaluee may not have a treating physician who knows his condition well enough to describe it. With a suggestion from the evaluator, the attorney may assist in collecting the health information essential to a vocational evaluation by commissioning an independent medical examination (IME) from a physician with the requisite specialty. The independent medical examiner can specify a diagnosis and prognosis to help the evaluator and trier of fact make a determination of disability. The attorney often has information about the availability of health insurance or financial resources for the independent medical examination.

Exploring the extent of potential work disability can bring up strong feelings in both parties and the attorneys, especially if it is likely that the evaluee will be identified as too disabled to work. This eventuality could place a difficult financial burden on the supporting spouse.

If there are no responses from the evaluee's physicians or no medical verification of the disability is possible, the report should note that this problem has occurred, with documentation of the efforts to gain the information, and state conclusions that encompass both the possibilities that the evaluee is disabled and is not.

It is essential also for the evaluator not to exaggerate the potential occupational impact of the normal aches and pains of adults and thereby build an unsupported case for work disability or encourage hypochondria. The evaluator balances listening sympathetically for health issues with the awareness that many adults manage a work life while living with less than perfect health.

WHAT HEALTH INFORMATION IS NEEDED

Medical information for a vocational evaluation is narrowly targeted to the questions of work-related restrictions and how much or what kinds of functioning is possible.

The inquiry into medical impairment and work disability is not a broad investigation into the evaluee's general medical history. The evaluator does not need, and should not request, full medical records, treatment histories, or physician's notes. Because the dissolution is a matter of public record, and because the evaluator's file is subject to subpoena, information obtained can be submitted to the court, be part of settlement documents, or made available to the opposing party. For the vocational evaluation, the only medical information sought should be targeted to understanding work and work ability.

The requests for medical information ask about present conditions and those projected to be ongoing. Past treatments, surgeries, illnesses, conditions, and diagnoses that caused no major ongoing functional impairment, work disabilities, or activity restrictions are not applicable to the determination of functional capacity.

QUESTIONS FOR PHYSICIANS ABOUT A POTENTIALLY DISABLED EVALUEE

Physicians with relevant knowledge about the evaluee's functional capacity can write a letter or speak to the evaluator, but they often do not know what information is necessary to compare physical capacity to job demands.

Forms with the following questions can be handed to the evaluee, with a signed release of information form, to present to any physician who is familiar with the evaluee's condition, such as primary care physicians and specialist doctors, psychologists and psychiatrists, chiropractors, Licensed Clinical Social Workers (LCSWs) and Marriage & Family Therapists (MFTs), and other therapists. Answers to these questions help clarify a party's capacity to work without intruding into the doctor/patient relationship unnecessarily.

A. Diagnosis, prognosis

B. Has the patient reached maximum improvement? If no, when will this occur?

C. Can the patient work full time? If no, how many hours per day? Per week?

D. Does the patient have any restrictions in activities due to the diagnosis? If yes, describe, including the projected duration of the restrictions.

E. Does the patient take any medications? If yes, describe.

F. Do the medications restrict the patient's ability to work? If yes, describe, including the expected duration of the restrictions.

G. Comments and signature/date.

If the potentially disabling condition needs further description to determine how much work a person can do, the physician can complete a Functional Capacities Form (see Appendix I). The Functional Capacities Form is helpful, for instance, in clarifying lifting limits, standing and sitting times, and similar restrictions.

If further information is required about a person's psychological symptoms and mental functioning, and their impact on possible work, a longer list is in Appendix J.

HEALTH ISSUES OF A CHILD

I have a special needs kid and I have no idea how I can work and still give him all the help he has to have just to get through his day. His medical problems are so frequent and so complicated and they change all the time. His father doesn't get it. He thinks I just drop him off at school and then I lounge around all day till I pick him up.

The Family Law Code mandates consideration of a child's needs and their potential influence on the parental ability to work. One section refers to the custodial parent's ability to work without unduly interfering with the interests of dependent children. All children require parental care, but a child with special needs may demand so much more care that parental employment is questionable.

A parent of a special needs child may have to assist the vocational evaluator in understanding the child's condition, by bringing the medical questionnaire to the child's physicians and treatment providers. The parent also signs a release of information form.

To understand a child's special needs and the effect of those needs on the custodial parent's work capacity, the evaluator may consult with many people. For children diagnosed in preschool and school age, the school district usually has a primary responsibility to evaluate the child and get professional recommendations for the education of a child with special needs. These remediation services are the contents of an Individual Education Plan (IEP), a program individually created by specialists for the school district to educate a child with special needs. In addition to seeing the IEP, a vocational evaluator may get important information from professionals who work with the child, including:

- Pediatrician

- Physician specialists for the specific disability

- Speech therapist

- Occupational therapist

- Psychologist or psychotherapist

- Teacher, tutor, and IEP aide

- Regional Center (providing services and supports to individuals with developmental disabilities)

Children with developmental disabilities including mental retardation, cerebral palsy, epilepsy, autism, and similar conditions receive care coordinated by the California Department of Developmental Services or similar state agencies. The agency provides services and supports through state-operated developmental centers and community facilities, and contracts with 21 nonprofit regional centers. The regional centers serve as a local resource to help find and access the services and supports available to individuals with developmental disabilities and their families.

All or some of the supportive services can be appropriate sources of information about the time and activity demands a child's care can place on a parent.

| QUESTIONS FOR PHYSICIANS ABOUT A POTENTIALLY DISABLED CHILD |

Just as medical or psychological questions about an adult evaluee focus on the person's ability to work, questions about a child's health should focus on the impact the child's health condition on the parent's ability to work.

A. Diagnosis for [child], prognosis

B. Special treatment needs, (e.g., speech therapy, occupational therapy, physical therapy, behavior therapy, extra medical appointments, lab testing)

C. Does coordination of [child]'s medical care and/or special education require extra time of custodial parent? If yes, how many hours does this require? Expected duration of this time requirement?

D. Does custodial parent have to do treatments or supervise at-home special needs treatments? If yes, how many hours does this require? Expected duration of this time requirement?

E. Does [child]'s personal care require extra time from custodial parent? If yes, how many hours does this require? Expected duration of this time requirement?

F. Comments and signature/date.

THE CONSEQUENCES OF DISABILITY IN VOCATIONAL EVALUATIONS

A vocational evaluator's expert opinion that a person's disability limits her or his ability to work can have an effect on the amount and/or the duration of support if the trier of fact accepts the conclusions as valid. If the evaluee's condition is severe enough, it can also constitute a reason to change custody arrangements. The fear of lost custody sometimes prevents evaluees from claiming that a medical problem may keep them from working full or part time, because they are concerned that the opposing spouse will use the argument that inability to work indicates inability to care for the children.

In the field of vocational evaluation, the facts that a person cannot attend a work place reliably, that their skills are not marketable, or that their physical and mental abilities are impaired are primary issues. The vocational evaluator cannot overlook or ignore them at the request of an attorney or other interested party. The trier of fact makes the final decision about the amount of work expected of the evaluated spouse. The evaluator has the responsibility to reveal all issues germane to that decision and proffer background information so that decisions of the trier of fact are based on complete data.

In an agreed or court-ordered evaluation, the vocational evaluator does not have the option to omit any material that informs the question of employability, no matter how inconvenient it is for one side or the other. It is not the neutral evaluator's function to assist one party's attorney in concealing a significant fact from the other party.

The only situation in which omitting health information relevant to vocational outcomes is an appropriate action is if the attorney hires the evaluator as a consultant, not as an expert. In this retention arrangement, the evaluator has the option to reveal the existence of a disability that could be detrimental to the attorney's client solely to the attorney; the evaluation is work product and the attorney decides what to do with the information. However, once an attorney declares the evaluator as an expert in the case, even though retained by one side, the evaluation and its conclusions are potentially open to all sides of the case.

This is true no matter which party may have increased financial responsibility because of the disability. If a supported spouse is disabled, the supporting spouse may have longer support burdens. If a custodial parent's disability is severe, custody arrangements may be readjusted to ensure the welfare of the child.

Not addressing the issue of disability in a vocational evaluation report may have long-term financial consequences that are the opposite of what is expected or intended. The evaluator may note that the evaluee has described a health concern but not describe the impact of that concern in the vocational conclusions. If the evaluator does not explore whether an existing medical or psychological problem rises to the level of a disability and creates a barrier to employment, the judge or mediator may assume that this omission indicates that no disability exists. The support decision based on this assumption may impute income to the disabled spouse or require her or him to seek work.

Sometimes the disabled spouse returns to court to ask for an extension of support, demonstrating no income and (re)describing the disability. Alternatively, the supporting spouse returns to court, asking for a reduction of support due to noncompliance with the seek work order. (A seek work order is an official notice from the court to a party that he or she is expected to hunt for a job.) A second vocational evaluation may reveal that the disability exists, has existed since the first evaluation, and has been the reason for the disabled spouse's not working. All of this expense, disappointment, and conflict could be avoided if the first evaluation accurately described a health issue that interferes with work.

◆◆◆

Addressing the question of health fairly is an essential part of a vocational evaluation.

Age to me means nothing. I can't get old; I'm working. As long as you're working, you stay young.

George Burns (1896-1996), comedian

ABILITY TO WORK – AGE

Vocational evaluators consider the age of the evaluees in all vocational examinations. Individuals' physical capacities change over decades, as do their interests, knowledge, and skills. Evaluees referred for divorce-related evaluations in their fifties and sixties often have significant fears about whether they can find acceptance in the work world at their ages. A common question is whether a person 55 or over, considered an older worker, has an earning capacity at all, and if so, to what extent.

No one is going to hire me with my gray hair and wrinkles. The people interviewing me are younger than my kids. They won't hire someone old enough to be their grandparent.

The California Family Law Code (Section 4320a[2]) demonstrates an understanding that, for someone who spent major time in childcare rather than at work, the loss of work opportunity may require compensation. The law states that a factor in determining earning capacity is the "extent to which the supported party's present or future earnings are impaired by periods of unemployment that were incurred during the marriage to permit the supported party to devote time to domestic duties." Puzzella (CA 2000) states that provision enables the court specifically to protect the supported spouse who is older. The older spouse may have few marketable skills and diminished future employment opportunities because of his or her long absence from the labor force. "Experts are essential to establish the magnitude of the supported or caregiving spouse's career losses in situations of this type."

The Reynolds (CA 1998) case addresses the questions of age and retirement. The appeals court held that it cannot attribute a monthly income to an older supporting spouse based on his potential ability to earn rather than on his actual earnings, if the attribution would require him to work well past the "generally accepted retirement age of 65." The Reynolds court held that no one may be compelled to work after the usual retirement age of 65 in order to pay the same amount of spousal support as when he was employed. Just as a married couple may expect a reduction in income due to retirement, a divorced spouse cannot expect to receive the same high amount of support after the supporting spouse retires, so a supporting spouse should not be forced to continue working if there is a bona fide retirement. Under those circumstances, the trial court may determine that there has been a material change in circumstances to justify a modification of support. The Reynolds case states that the court cannot apply an imputed "capacity to earn" standard to a person with a bona fide retirement.

105

In addition, the Schmir case (CA 2005) required the supported spouse to make good faith efforts to become employed only to age 65.

With Social Security's full retirement age (Social Security Administration) rising from 65 to 66 and soon to 67 for those born in 1960 and later, many older people will want to work past 65, or need to, to maximize the retirement income they receive. There are other reasons why older workers will, and will want to, remain in the work force.

- The recession of 2008-2011 and its layoffs have forced many older workers into retiring earlier than they had planned or could afford. They must return to work for financial reasons.

- The declines in housing values and the stock market have eaten into the savings many older workers counted on for retirement income.

- The increased costs of health insurance have made employment a more stable and affordable source of medical insurance coverage for employees under 65 who are not eligible for Medicare.

- Defined benefit pensions are less common and retirement savings are often in investments whose returns may not meet the costs of retirement living.

- People are living longer and will want to continue meaningful activity into their senior years. Women who reach age 65 can expect to live another 20 years, men another 15 years. (GAO, 2005)

- With an increase in computer use, jobs have become physically less demanding in the last several decades, making working possible for older people. (Johnson, Mermin & Resseger, 2007) Approximately 11 percent of occupations require only sedentary–the lightest level–strength. (Truthan, 2003-2007)

- In family law cases, healthy older individuals who have divorced may be starting new families with younger spouses, changing motivation from retirement to staying active and earning income past normal retirement age.

The outlook for employment opportunities for older workers is mixed. Older employers view workers in their own age cohort positively for many worker traits. They see older workers as having a good work ethic and steady attendance, the ability to get along with others, supervisory experience, and possession of valuable experience, specialized skills, and knowledge. Employers may also see older workers as being less adept at computers, not able to learn quickly, and likely to feel entitled to higher wages and positions

Both federal and state laws prohibit discrimination in employment against older workers. The Age Discrimination in Employment Act of 1967 (ADEA) protects certain applicants and employees 40 years of age and older from discrimination on the basis of age in hiring, promotion, discharge, compensation, or the terms, conditions, or privileges of employment. The ADEA is enforced by the Equal Employment Opportunity Commission (EEOC).

California's Fair Employment and Housing Act (FEHA) prohibits employment discrimination, harassment, and retaliation based upon many conditions including being age 40 or older. The passage of antidiscrimination laws does not mean that such discrimination does not occur. In fact, the existence of the laws is evidence that such discrimination is widespread enough that employees in these classes require legal protection. Documentation of cases or trends in job categories of age discrimination is hard to gather, as employers are not likely to admit to turning down an applicant because of age or inclined to create written evidence of these decisions.

If the vocational evaluator feels that age discrimination is likely to occur in the work reentry attempts in spite of antidiscrimination laws, she or he should describe why this might be. For instance, in occupations that usually involve significant overtime, or heavy physical demands, employers may assume an older worker would not be able to perform the tasks, whether or not that assumption is true for the individual. Stereotypical ideas about what kind of person can do a job are common. A computer network systems administrator is frequently pictured as a socially awkward young man. Older workers may not be hired for such jobs or envision themselves in them.

Demographics will influence the movement of older workers into the labor force as the baby boomer generation reaches its sixties, pushing the median age of the labor force higher. This trend is projected to continue during the decade of 2008 through 2018. (Toosi, 2009) Persons 55 and older participate in the labor market at a record rate of more than 40 percent, (BLS, 2010) normalizing the presence of older workers on the job. More than half of workers 65 and older work full time rather than part time. (BLS, 2008) While older workers tend not to be laid off as readily as younger ones, once they have lost jobs, older workers find it takes more time to obtain employment than it does for younger workers. Health is a major concern for older workers considering returning to work. This aspect of a person's life may supersede the impact of age.

The consideration of age for a vocational evaluation, therefore, cannot be a blanket proposition that, say, everyone over a certain age is unable to work or find employment. The conclusions about earning capacity for an older worker must be as individualized as they are for younger workers. The vocational evaluator combines the influence of age with attention to the evaluee's health and cognitive abilities, intelligence and willingness to learn, prior work experience and knowledge of work-related information and skills, geography and transportation options, financial need, familial support and resources, physical demands of their desired occupations, and similar personal qualities that the older evaluee brings to work.

Age can have a direct influence on the shape of the vocational conclusions. For instance, a vocational plan for a 60-year-old should probably not call for a protracted period of further education that postpones work reentry for multiple years. Older workers may have fewer types of jobs open to them if they must have sedentary work rather than a job requiring prolonged standing, such as retail sales, or one requiring repeated lifting. Older workers may want to avoid extensive travel demands from a job, though some may find such travel acceptable because travel no longer interferes with family responsibilities. A vocational plan for an older worker may have to anticipate a longer job search, and a period of computer skill training to increase his or her competitive advantage.

Age by itself is insufficient to find a person unable to work or to be employable. In combination with other factors such as lack of ability to attain skills, poor health, language barriers, or such an extended absence from the labor market that an employer is unlikely to hire, advanced age can be decisive in converting an employment problem into a significant barrier to achieving an earning capacity.

ABILITY TO WORK – WORKING AND CHILDCARE

We made an agreement when we got married that he would support the family and I'd stay home with the kids. It was important to both of us that the children would be raised by us, not by strangers, and that essentially means by me. My kids have never had to go to childcare after school.

Many parents participating in a vocational evaluation have not experienced the complicated juggling required for working and caring for children at the same time. It is common for them to fear making the transition from full time parent to working parent.

I'm running from morning to night now taking care of the kids. I barely have any time for myself. I have no idea how I'm going to add a full time job to this kind of schedule.

Parents without a separate income do not feel unemployed; they feel their schedules are filled with running a household, managing children's schedules of school, sports, and play dates, and volunteering in activities that support their children's schools or sports programs. They often coordinate home repair projects or remodeling, selling and buying a house, planning and executing household moves, paying bills, and other important home tasks.

The complications of coordinating childcare and work are not experienced only by nonworking mothers. Often fathers have jobs with out-of-town travel, extended hours to 60 to 70 per week, or significant amounts of work-related evening activity, so that prior to the divorce they have not spent much one-on-one time with their children beyond planned vacations. With a transition to shared custody, fathers who worked many hours often spend more time with their children as a divorced parent than they did while married.

The default assumption in family law is that a healthy parent whose child does not have special needs will be able to work. While difficult, and perhaps requiring some adjustments in expectations, the majority of parents work. Employment patterns in the United States from the

Bureau of Labor Statistics show that as of 2008, 71 percent of mothers with children under age 18 participated in the labor market. (BLS, 2010).

Of mothers with older children, 6 to 17 years of age, 77.5 percent were in the labor force, compared with 63.6 percent of mothers with younger children. In 2008, 76 percent of unmarried mothers were in the labor force, compared with 69 percent of married mothers. A National Association of Child Care Resource and Referral Agencies report (NACCRRA, 2010) noted that 64 percent of mothers with children under age 6 are in the workforce.

For parents with children with health problems or other special needs, the California Family Law Code mandates consideration of a child's needs and their potential influence on the parental ability to work. Incorporating caring for dependent children with special needs into the vocational evaluation is discussed in the Health and Disability section earlier in Chapter 6.

CHILDCARE COSTS

For parents with either a child under elementary school age or multiple children, costs of childcare can rise steeply. Most of the post-tax income of a working parent could be spent on childcare, especially if the parent is starting in a low-paying job. Childcare cost considerations can affect the timing of work reentry, share of childcare costs, and the choice of career.

NACCRRA's report found that parents in most states, including California, are paying more for a year of childcare than they would for a year of public university education.

In California in 2010, the average cost of infant care is $11,300. For a preschooler, it is about $7,800. Nationally, the annual costs for full-time care for an infant range from $4,560 to $18,773; for a child in preschool, $4,460 to $13,158; and for before- and after-school care for a school-age child $2,451 to $10,400.

Example A) If a family with two children, one in preschool and another in elementary school, must pay for child care, costs in northern California could equal $6,500 to $7,000 for the younger child and $2,600 to $3,000 annually for the older child, totaling $9,100 to $10,000, or $758 to $833 monthly.

A reentry worker who transitions from full-time parent to working, for example, as a medical secretary in San Francisco's East Bay counties could expect to earn mean gross wages of $19.05 per hour, or $39,623 annually. (CA EDD, 2011) If 33 percent of the gross income is deducted for taxes, the worker receives a net income of $26,547 or $2,212 monthly. Childcare costs around $800 to $1000 per month can consume a large portion of income at this level.

After deducting normal work expenses such as transportation and commute costs, meals, clothing, and parking, the financial benefits of working become less compelling for workers with incomes and expenses similar to those in the example above. The informal cost/benefit analysis that runs through the thoughts of a reentry worker contrasts the minimal financial benefit with the hassles of managing schedules, learning new skills, finding a job, and responding to the demands of both family and boss. The positives become much less obvious. This is especially true for someone who is unsure of a job goal, has fewer skills or no recent work experience, or who is fearful and anxious about working generally.

Not all the benefits of work are financial, however, and vocational planning for the parent of young children will want to take into account other life concerns. Does the parent need to work almost full time to have health insurance? Does the parent lack a degree, skill training, certification, internship or other pre-vocational experience to qualify for the chosen vocation? How long should this pre-employment training take? What will be the negative impact on future employability if the parent stays longer out of the labor market? What positives, such as increased confidence and self-esteem, opportunities for professional networking, and adult social contacts, will result from working?

The vocational evaluation can lay out these questions for the evaluee to consider in planning a career and the trier of fact to consider in defining appropriate support.

Some ways to accommodate child care costs in vocational planning:

- If the reentry parent requires training, schedule part time education while the children are young, to minimize childcare costs and parent/child separation.

- Extend the training period for the parent of a very young child to coordinate reentry into full time work at the time when the child leaves pre-school for elementary school.

- Accommodate work to manage after-school care with flexible scheduling or part time hours.

- Adjust full time work schedules in four 8-10 hour shifts per week rather than five, or incorporate work from home.

- Arrange custody so that the reentry parent loses fewer work hours and spends less on childcare.

In general, if the parent is expecting to reenter the work world, a shorter time away from the labor market will be less detrimental to the future job search and prospects of being hired. If the parent must spend more time not working while taking care of children because of the age of the children and the cost of their care, she can use some of the intervening time until they are old enough for school for pre-vocational and career preparation activities.

Some beneficial preemployment experiences are enrolling in school programs, increasing work skills in online courses, taking weekend seminars, volunteering in a work-related activity, participating in an unpaid internship, connecting to professional organizations, serving with nonprofit groups, or helping in a friend's business activities.

ABILITY TO WORK – CULTURAL DIFFERENCES

The vocational options of people not born in the United States are as varied as the evaluees themselves. In a recent analysis of 520 family law evaluations done in California, 10 percent concerned divorcing spouses born outside the United States. In this discussion, only the employment prospects for immigrants with the legal right to work are considered.

The foreign-born population in the United States comes from all over the world. The largest group of immigrants, almost half of the foreign-born population of the United States, is Hispanic or Latino, with roots in Mexico and other Latin American countries. In 2000, more than one-quarter of the foreign-born population came from Mexico. The next largest group comes from countries in Asia. The third largest group comes from Africa. Others come from Europe. (Center for Adult English Language Acquisition) Almost 30 percent of California's population is foreign born; New York's population is more than 20 percent foreign born. (Migration Policy Institute, 2010) Even states without a large percentage of people not born in the United States have pockets of immigrants. For example, the top three countries of birth of the foreign born in Illinois were Mexico, Poland, and India. The majority of individuals who speak a language other than English at home speak Spanish (60 percent). The number of Spanish speakers is more than 10 times the number of individuals who speak the second most prevalent language, Chinese. The remaining eight of the top 10 languages spoken are (in this order): French, German, Tagalog, Vietnamese, Italian, Korean, Russian, and Polish.

The evaluator will want to understand the cultural expectations about work and job search that a foreign-born evaluee brings to the prospect of work reentry. The idea of an adult choosing a career based on interests may be a new concept. In some countries, vocational choice is determined in high school or earlier; in others, jobs are chosen by parents, by the government, or for the highest possible wages.

Some women who work expect to remain in well-defined roles connected to home and children. Roles beyond that may be hard to envision. Some foreign-born job seekers have never learned how to look for work or how to describe their skills and other vocational assets to an interviewer. They need job-seeking skill training and cultural information that, for instance, being assertive is culturally appropriate in the United States. Cultural sensitivity is an essential evaluator trait.

I can't tell my family back home that I'm getting a divorce. I'm a 35-year-old woman without a husband, without children, and without a job. My parents would be so ashamed; they couldn't even tell anyone in the family what has happened to me. I feel like a complete failure and I have nothing to offer an employer.

For people not born in the United States, a major concern for employment evaluation is English language skill. Some people residing in the United States who were not United States citizens at birth have lived in the country many years and attended American schools. For those with language skills close to those of native speakers of English, employment opportunities are unlimited by communication difficulties. Learning English involves four basic skills —reading, writing, speaking, and listening. Speaking and listening are often the most important skills that English language learners need to develop to meet their immediate needs.

Initially, the evaluator may want to engage the services of a translator for the initial structured interview to ensure that the evaluee understands questions accurately and the evaluator has a clear picture of the evaluee's background. However, a person whose command of English is insufficient to speak one-on-one to the attentive interviewer will probably be constrained to employment within her or his language community. For those who are less adept at using English, the best suggestion for widening work opportunities is to increase their language knowledge. Unless the foreign-born evaluee only wants to work within her own cultural group, she will need to develop the best degree of English usage allowed by her education, intelligence, and learning ability to maximize her success in an American labor market.

Employment not requiring much English language ability is limited. Some examples of jobs done by monolingual speakers of languages other than English include retail sales in a small grocery in an ethnic neighborhood and teaching in a non-English-speaking school. Often positions not requiring much English require more physical capacity than communication skills, such as food production, cleaning and janitorial work, personal care, medical care, childcare, and some computer work.

Generally, positions requiring little English pay at the lower end of the wage scale. The availability of these jobs will vary by the demands and size of the ethnic population in the area. Labor market research about jobs in non-English communities may be contracted to a speaker of the specific language to determine job availability, necessary skills, and compensation ranges within that language-defined community.

A common question is whether an adult can learn enough English within a reasonable period to change earning capacity significantly. The answer to this can influence whether a vocational plan should incorporate English as a Second Language (ESL) training as an element, with extended time allotted for language acquisition. The amount of time it takes an adult to learn English varies from person to person and depends on such factors as the individual's age, educational background, level of literacy in the native language, and opportunities to interact with native English speakers.

The questions about English skills an evaluator will want to examine are:

- What grade of education did the evaluee finish in his or her native language? If the evaluee is not literate in his or her own language, it will be harder to acquire a significant increase in English skills.

- How motivated is the evaluee and how well does she understand the link between English skills and higher wages? A variety of emotional issues such as self-confidence, anxiety, and motivation influence language acquisition, especially speaking.

- How old is the evaluee? While children learn languages more easily than adults, adults who have learned one language well and have an understanding of grammatical structure can transfer this knowledge to learning English. The ability to learn a foreign language does not have an age drop-off point; rather, language learning ability declines gradually with age.

- How long will it take the evaluee to increase his or her English ability? It is generally accepted that it takes from 5-7 years to go from not knowing any English at all to being able to accomplish most communication tasks including academic tasks. To reach a basic level of comprehension, research indicates that it would take from 500 to 1000 hours of instruction for an adult who is literate in her native language, but has had no prior English instruction, to reach a level where she can satisfy her basic needs, survive on the job, and have limited social interaction in English. (Collier, 1989)

- How much contact does the evaluee have, or is willing to have, with English speakers to increase his opportunity to acquire conversation skills, both in understanding and speaking? Many foreign-born evaluees who have been in the United States for years can read and write some English, but still spend much of their time with others who speak their native language, not with English speakers. It may require a change in friendship patterns and some discomfort for the English language learner to get more exposure to spoken English.

One source of information about the evaluee's language skills beyond the interview conversation is English as a Second Language (ESL) testing in a local adult school or other community facility that offers ESL training. It is helpful to know the evaluee's tested English level.

There are seven levels of ESL training, (DHHS, 1985) starting with Level 1, for those with no English at all, to Level 7, advanced English. Level 1 covers the alphabet, numbers, and beginning vocabulary; Level 3 teaches listening, speaking, reading, and writing skills to function satisfactorily in most real-life situations related to immediate needs. Level 5 students learn skills needed to function effectively in both familiar and unfamiliar social situations and familiar work situations. At this level, the students gain the communication skills needed to discuss and interpret cultural differences and use English to solve problems outside the class. Finishing Level 7 allows the student to demonstrate knowledge of written and spoken English well enough to pass the Test of English as a Foreign Language (TOEFL) and/or participate in a college or university program.

Knowing how skilled the evaluee's English is at the time of the evaluation enables the evaluator to estimate the duration of ESL training that could make a significant difference in earning capacity.

With answers to these and similar questions, an evaluator can decide which vocational options to recommend and whether the vocational plan will include ESL training. The evaluator may offer two or more alternatives, one job for in which the evaluee's current English skills qualify her or him that may pay less, and another, longer plan to acquire more English skills to qualify for jobs that could pay more.

Evaluees who were educated in another country can get help in knowing how U.S. colleges or businesses will view their foreign training. Bringing a transcript to the school's counseling office is a good starting point. Many universities hire Articulation Officers who review the records of students transferring credits from another institution to the school. The Articulation Officer informs the incoming student which of his or her past classes or degrees will satisfy the requirements of the school and be accepted for credit.

For education documents not written in English, online services that evaluate educational credentials will translate each educational course, credential, credit, and grade from high school and undergraduate studies into the corresponding United States experience. These advisory services compare the student's credentials with their American educational equivalents and give the student an advisory document designed to help academic institutions, licensing boards and employers in the United States understand foreign credentials. If the evaluee knows which school she wants to attend, she will want to ask which credential evaluation services are acceptable to the school.

◆ ◆ ◆

Helping foreign-born evaluees understand how to negotiate a path into the U.S. work world requires cultural awareness and an understanding of opportunities that may fall outside the evaluator's personal cultural experience. Using culturally appropriate resources can bridge this gap.

I like work; it fascinates me. I can sit and look at it for hours.

Jerome K. Jerome, *Three Men in a Boat*

LABOR MARKET RESEARCH

An essential service in vocational evaluations, labor market research creates evidence of the second major component of the definition of earning capacity, the "opportunity to work." This analysis of the work world answers questions about the availability of specific positions and their associated compensation ranges. Starting with a basic methodology, evaluators apply a flexible approach to performing the research and understanding its results, necessitated by the wide variability of job types they study.

It is essential for labor market research to be current and based on fact so that significant expert information informs the trier of fact.

LEGAL BASIS FOR LABOR MARKET RESEARCH

California Family Law Code sections establish the need for and the parameters of labor market information by calling for an assessment of the "current availability of employment opportunities" to determine "the party's ability to obtain employment that would allow the party to maintain herself or himself at the marital standard of living."

That ability, or earning capacity, of the party refers both to the marketable skills of the supported party and to the job market for those skills.

Case law in California family law has found that there must be proof that a person has an earning capacity, even if they are not earning at that level at the time. If the need for this proof is met, income can be imputed to the spouse. The cases of Regnery, Bardzik, and Wittgrove are most relevant.

The Regnery (CA 1989) case establishes the requirement to show ability and opportunity to work. The summary in Bardzik (CA 2008) includes a description of the case law that forms the mandate for performing labor market research.

The Bardzik (CA 2008) court stated that if one parent seeks to use imputed income to modify an existing support order, the parent seeking imputation bears the burden of proof. He or she must show that the other parent has the ability and opportunity to earn that imputed income. In

Wittgrove (CA 2004), the court stated that there can be no imputation of income if the parent seeking the order failed to present any competent evidence the other parent had the ability or opportunity to earn imputed income.

The labor market research allows the parent who carries the burden of proof to meet that burden by providing competent evidence that the parent to whom earnings are imputed has the opportunity to earn.

What constitutes competent evidence may vary, but it must have some basis in fact. In the case of Cohn (CA 1998), the appellate court reversed the finding of imputed income for insufficient evidence to support the finding as to the amount of income imputed: "[F]igures for earning capacity cannot be drawn from thin air; they must have some tangible evidentiary foundation."

QUESTIONS THAT CAN BE ANSWERED BY LABOR MARKET RESEARCH

Generally, the term *occupation* refers to a group of similar jobs; *job* refers to an individual position with an employer.

Typical questions that require search of the labor market for evidence of opportunity to work often fall into these categories.

General labor market conditions

- The unemployment rate state-wide and for a local geographic area

- The emergence of a new occupation or the phasing out of an old one

- The reasonable commute length /distance to a work site

Job demand and employer requirements

- Labor market competition nationally or locally for an occupation

- The existence of an occupation within a reasonable commute distance

- Availability of current job openings within a reasonable geographic distance

- The experience, education, licenses, certificates, degrees, and personal qualities required to obtain and perform the job

- The tasks and skills needed to perform the job

- The physical and psychological demands of the job

- The work conditions of the typical job in a specific field

- The common requirements in an occupation for travel or extended hours

- The employer-preferred sources of training and experience for the job

Salaries and compensation

- Wages for a particular occupation, skill set, or job level

- The likely salary range associated with the chosen job

- The benefits and compensation styles associated with the job

- The probable earnings at varying years of experience

Job search

- In what industries the job exists and how an applicant makes contact with potential employers

- How long it would take to obtain a job in the chosen field

- The appropriate methods for finding and obtaining a job in the chosen field

- What steps are involved to conduct a good faith job search for the job

DEMONSTRATING OPPORTUNITY TO WORK

Opportunity is missed by most because it is dressed in overalls and looks like work.

Thomas A. Edison

The ideal way to show that someone has an opportunity to work is to have a valid job offer made to the person who will actually be working in the job. This is almost never possible. If a researcher phones an employer and asks, *"If a person with the following experience interviewed for your open job, would you hire her?"* no employer would respond with a definite affirmative answer. Employers do not hire a job candidate sight unseen and will never state a willingness to hire an unknown applicant. They express fears that such a statement could hold them legally liable. Even an applicant whose resume matches the employer's requirements exactly must go through personal interviews. The research about job availability and opportunity for an actual evaluee candidate therefore rarely results in this ideal confirmation.

Employers' natural caution in stating a firm commitment to hire an unknown candidate turns demonstrating opportunity for employment into a hypothetical proposition, unless the evaluee is currently working (and sometimes not even then). The expert uses judgment and experience with employment patterns to form expert opinions. This is especially true in researching opportunities for an applicant who has not sought employment and who may still need to acquire the skills to qualify for hiring. The task of demonstrating opportunity to work involves matching employer requirements as closely as possible to an applicant's background, but cannot become a guarantee that a certain evaluee will find work.

The researcher of work opportunities matches the research questions to the evaluee's background and experience. The researcher can target a group of connected jobs, and needs to drill down past the broad occupational level to make relevant distinctions within an occupational group.

For example, labor market research for a driver would differentiate between local drivers and long-haul truckers, shuttle drivers and municipal bus drivers, taxi drivers and school bus drivers, delivery drivers and drivers of 16-wheelers. Similarly, labor market research for teachers would distinguish between teachers in elementary, middle, and high schools, multi-subject and single subject expertise, credential-holding or not, public or private schools, college level or below, bilingual or special education.

The time spent on labor market research and data compilation reflects the complexity of the practice, which varies according to multiple features of the assignment, including the job goal, geography, and the employment climate.

LABOR MARKET RESEARCH METHODS

Using multiple sources and more than one type of information maximizes the positive aspects of each and allows the evaluator to crosscheck results across sources. The reliance on several sources is the "tangible evidentiary foundation" of the conclusions in expert vocational examinations. The method is to collect enough data to support the conclusion for a likely outcome, using several different methods, if possible, to demonstrate opportunity.

Vocational experts Neulicht, Gann, Berg, and Taylor (2007) studied the practices of forensic vocational experts nationally on how they conduct labor market research. They found that "relatively little information related to the protocols for conducting a Labor Market Survey is available" and "No standardized methodology exists on what protocol represents best practice or how the method utilized relates to the scientific process."

The authors found that the current practice to conduct labor market research by established forensic vocational experts is predominantly (82 percent of the respondents) to find labor market data by two methods:

- The more commonly used approach was to research data in published research and statistical data in printed or internet resources from directories, U.S. Bureau of Labor

118

Statistics, U.S. Census Bureau, state or federal employment statistics databases, online job listings, or placement services.

- Employer sampling— personal contacts with employers, their representatives, recruiters, and individuals from professional or trade associations, unions, training programs, or others with knowledge of hiring trends—was the less common research approach.

Collating and comparing multiple data points results in information that will describe the conditions that the job seeker will actually confront as closely as possible. Combining sources of labor market information builds toward greater accuracy and reliability of the expert opinion. The expert decides which sources to use, and how much weight to give to each according to the individual job in question. The professional judgment of the evaluator and the largest possible amount of research, given the time and financial constraints of the assignment, will make the information most useful for the trier of fact and the attorneys.

LABOR MARKET RESEARCH RESULTS

- To demonstrate job availability and employer requirements, the labor market research results in a list of actual job openings posted publicly, or, through employer sampling, described by individual employers, with employer requirements for comparison to the skills, experience, and knowledge held by the evaluee.

Employer requirements in posted job openings give a good idea of the criteria they will use for hiring, but it is rare for a candidate to have all of the listed qualities and experience. Job posting requirements are often an employer's "wish list" rather than a required checklist. Employers will often hire someone who lacks some training if the applicant has other qualities that conform to their needs. Job listings showing employer requirements that are evidence of general hiring in the field and thus opportunity to work for the evaluee may not exactly match the evaluee's background; this does not necessarily demonstrate that the evaluee is not a viable candidate for the jobs.

For instance, the job listings may not match the ideal commute distance for the evaluee's preferences, depending on which jobs are open at the time of the research. Or the evaluee may not know all the software listed by the employer, have the exact education preferred, or have prior experience in the precise segment of the industry. The job listings may not be ideal in the eyes of the evaluee who may be thinking concretely about whether a specific job fits. The evaluator uses the listing to determine trends.

- To demonstrate earnings at the time of next employment and in the longer term, the research results indicate salary data in the chosen industry. Salary information emerges from valid sources such as posted job openings, salary surveys, and published aggregate statistical data about job titles related to the evaluee's identified career.

Salary surveys focused on specific professions or industries are often excellent data sources for information about occupational wages within an industry. However, many salary surveys are not as narrowed geographically as the state data. The salary surveys conducted by professional organizations may show national averages, state or regional compensation statistics, but are less likely to differentiate at the county or city level.

Collecting data from several sources allows a reasonable approximation of a salary range.

- To demonstrate up-to-date and local information about employers' needs, employer sampling yields quotes from local employers about the present market conditions, hiring possibilities, salaries and qualification requirements.

The most geographically precise information is often gleaned by speaking to an employer who can discuss qualifications he or she finds essential to perform the job, the company's recent and projected hiring patterns, and salary ranges. These pieces of information are very informative but do not conform to the standards of a statistically random survey. The response comes from one employer, in a targeted location, at a single point in time, about a job title used by that employer. Whether the job is still open by the time of the report, whether the employer would interview the evaluee, or whether the employer would offer the job, are not knowable.

Because the employer sampling information is not a random sample, its broad applicability is a matter for the expert to determine, by comparing it to other information sources. The quality of the direct contact information depends on the speaker. The researcher may contact more employers to determine whether the information is true across the industry. The tradeoff for specificity and immediacy is the loss of validity and reliability, and perhaps widespread applicability of the responses.

UNDERSTANDING LABOR MARKET RESEARCH – STATISTICAL DATA

Large statistical databases of employment wages and employment incidence collected by governmental agencies such as the Bureau of Labor Statistics (BLS) and Employment Development Department (EDD) have the considerable advantages of well-established and published methodologies, consistency and availability of historical data, published levels of validity and reliability, and availability for a wide geographical spread. They provide the data for year-to-year comparisons, contrasts between states and counties or cities, and cover a large range of occupational titles.

Limitations inherent in such databases stem from the same size and spread of the information.

TIME DELAYS

Statistical data such as that developed by the state and local agencies can show numbers of jobs, employers, median and mean wages, and the mid-range (25th to 75th percentile) of wages. These data, grouped by county or metropolitan statistical areas covering multiple counties, list the job categories with the largest number of employees. They are typically published well after the data are collected; the lag time may make a significant difference in conclusions about job availability. The OES data come from a semiannual mail survey that samples about 37,000 establishments per year, taking 3 years to collect the full sample in California.

The time lag between data collection and data publication can make a significant difference in applicability of the data points. For an example, we can look at the California Employment Development Department's (EDD) Occupational and Employment Survey Statistics (OES) data posted for Contra Costa County in California. In the first quarter of 2010, the OES listed the estimates of numbers of employees in each job category using data from May 2008 and the mean and median wages earned by workers in those categories using data from the first quarter of 2009. However, the nation and California experienced a major depression with major job losses within the time scope of these data points. In May 2008, Contra Costa County's unemployment rate was 5.6 percent; in May 2009, it was 10 percent. (CA EDD, 2011). By the first quarter of 2010 when the OES data were accessed, California's unemployment rate was 12.4 percent. (CA EDD, 2010) Nationally, the unemployment rate was 5.0 percent in January 2008; in December 2009, it was 10.0 percent. The underemployment rate, which counts people whose hours have been cut along with those working part time for lack of full-time positions, reached 16.8 percent in February 2010.

With rapid major labor market shifts such as these, it may not be possible for a forensic expert to draw solid conclusions about job availability from data collected in 2008 and 2009 but published in 2010, even using data as reliable as those from government sources. However, no other data sources as reliable may be available.

JOB SPECIFICITY

The Employment Development Department's Occupational Employment Statistics (OES) data describe approximately 770 occupations, listed by Standard Occupational Classification (SOC) codes,[9] about half of the 1420 SOC codes. (CA EDD, 2011)

Because of the occupational coding, salary information from this and similar important sources may not apply precisely to the evaluee's situation. If an evaluee's chosen career falls into one of the defined job titles, such as kindergarten teacher or payroll clerk, the salaries relate more accurately. If the person works in a job not separately defined within the OES data, such as web content editor, the state's salary data may not research the occupation exactly or list it at all.

The OES data, while reliable and valid, also do not distinguish salaries for small geographic areas or cities. The state's data are shown for metropolitan statistical areas, metropolitan divisions, or "balance of state" regions that encompass two to seven counties in rural areas. The OES data reports list average wages across the counties and numbers of employers in the entire region, although the employment opportunities may not occur be equally distributed among the parts of the districts or regions, and salaries may differ significantly within the counties. Rural areas will have different employment patterns in job openings and even in pay ranges from urban areas, although information from both areas may fall within the same statistical grouping in the state's data.

The SOC codes derive data from employers of all sizes and length of time in business, from the largest multinational corporations to the small start-ups in niche markets. The SOC codes do not differentiate between related but separate jobs such as graphics designer, web designer, compositor, web software developer, and website manager— jobs that often require linked but different skills and levels of expertise and result in different wage estimates.

EXAMPLES OF THE LIMITATIONS OF THE LARGEST EMPLOYMENT INFORMATION DATABASES

While the OES data distinguish 44 categories of teachers, the database groups all elementary school teachers together and differentiates them only if they teach special education classes. It does not differentiate wages between private and public employers, faith-based or other private schools, by zip code or other demographic indicators.

All the 3,450 lawyers in California's Alameda and Contra Costa Counties (the Metropolitan Statistical Area MSA known as the Oakland-Fremont-Hayward Metropolitan Division) are grouped into a single code with a single mean wage. The broad range of attorney salaries is lumped into the general job title "Attorney" in the state's wage database, not separated by area of specialization, size of employer, or years of experience.

This statistical aggregation does not help the vocational expert distinguish between the earnings of the corporate litigator billing more than 2,000 hours per year at top rates from the earnings of the sole practitioner of public interest law working part-time in a shared office space. These professionals with the same education and license may differ in earnings by hundreds of thousands of dollars a year. The expert will want accurate differential predictions of income for attorneys who work for large litigation firms compared to those in small firms, for those who work as experienced in-house counsel versus those who are brand-new public defenders, those who work in intellectual property law and those who represent the disabled for their Social Security disability benefits. The expert seeks other, non-governmental salary data sources for distinct practice areas to separate these earnings more precisely.

Similarly, the 104,740 workers in Sales and Related Occupations listed in the EDD's OES data for the San Francisco Metropolitan Statistical Area (MSA) of San Francisco, San Mateo and

Marin Counties are listed in twenty categories. These twenty groups do not separate those who work full time or part time, earn commissions or are salaried, work in-house or on the road, or by other important distinguishing characteristics which can change earnings and working conditions significantly.

Thus, the published data from the most consistent government sources may not show enough detail for the vocational expert to project earnings with sufficient specificity to apply to the individual case. Other data sources, if available, must fill in the gaps.

DATA AVAILABILITY

Some occupations are well researched; others have no data collected about them at all. It is possible to find wage information for registered nurses (RNs), for instance, with wage information separated by city, employer type, responsibility level, job function, education, and years of experience. For the job of motorcycle salesperson, no published data are available at any level of specificity.

Commonly, jobs with a large number of employees working in the field that require licensing, certification, or formal training, or those covered by union contracts, are the subject of available labor market research. Occupations such as teacher, nurse, or physician are well described in labor market, as are marketers, and middle managers. Salaries of executives in public companies are known through the SEC filings. Salary data in occupations that are new and emerging, such as solar panel installer or blogger, or have few employees, such as winery marketer, are not as well documented. Those jobs that are mostly approached through less structured experience, such as artist or artists' representative, fabric designer, cookbook or travel writer, are not found in many published salary surveys or labor market databases. Some occupations and job titles that have little available wage data are those in which the majority of whose practitioners are self-employed, and those whose incomes are highly variable, such as hedge fund managers or forensic social workers.

GEOGRAPHIC SPECIFICITY

Statistical databases often cover a geographic spread that contains many areas that vary in pay and job availability. For evaluees living far from public transportation, the differentiation of job incidence and wages for openings within a reasonable commute may not be reflected in larger statistical databases.

For instance, the Society for Human Resource Management (SHRM) has compensation surveys for precise job titles within the industry – top corporate compensation and benefits executive, human resources (HR) manager, employee training manager, HR generalist, human resources information systems (HRIS) analyst, compensation analyst, employee training specialist, employment/recruiting representative, employees benefits administrator, and HR assistant – and lists compensation by levels of responsibility. Some data are national; some apply to regions or major cities, but data are not available for smaller cities or rural areas. These data points differentiate salaries by job titles well, but do not drill down geographically to find salary differences in small towns versus urban areas.

The OES data for the East Bay of San Francisco list wages collected in a large Metropolitan Division encompassing two counties. This blending of information does not permit a distinction in occupational wages between, say, the financially troubled city of Richmond (median household income $52,322) and, separated by only 20 miles, the more affluent town of Lafayette (median household income $123,152). (U.S. Census Bureau Data Set, 2008) This distinction is never one ignored by job seekers.

The data from the San Francisco-San Mateo-Redwood City Metropolitan Division, covering the counties of Marin, San Francisco, and San Mateo, do not separate the earnings of office clerks in San Francisco's financial district from those in rural western Marin County, although the pay levels vary as much as the temperature ranges. The OES's mid-range (25th percentile to 75th percentile) wages for office clerks, $12 per hour to almost $20, (annually $25,000 to $42,000), describe a range that is large enough to make a significant difference in family support calculations and quality of life. In this situation, it is important to understand small but relevant geographic regional differences to estimate an earning capacity.

These are the basic data sources for competent evidence to fulfill the burden of proving job availability and opportunity, but different jobs may necessitate diverse research methods to show opportunity.

UNDERSTANDING LABOR MARKET RESEARCH – EMPLOYER SAMPLING

Conversations with individual employers, representatives from professional organizations, schools, or recruiters can reveal helpful information not often studied in data surveys.

Some labor market information is searchable online through job listings in job search sites, through search firms or recruiters, from trade or professional organizations, or on individual employer websites. Information from these sources can yield these types of data:

- Job availability

- Job titles

- Job requirements for skills, knowledge, experience, training, licenses, education

- Pay levels and pay structures, e.g., salary or commission, benefits

- Hours of work

- Working conditions

- Methods of hiring and job access

- Frequency of openings and trends in job availability

Collected examples of multiple job listings reveal patterns of employer expectations and behavior.

From employer sampling, experts can learn about hiring practices, expectations of future hiring, subtle but important distinctions between experiential and educational backgrounds usual for successful job candidates, preferred training facilities, availability of disability accommodations, degree of competition for job openings, and the duration of the hiring procedure.

Information developed through personal one-on-one contacts has the advantage of reflecting actual demand for a particular job in a known location with precise details of what employers at a point in time seek in skill and experience. The possibility of generalizing such targeted data is a matter of expert judgment.

NONRANDOM SAMPLING

Employer sampling offers fascinating insights into businesses' viewpoints. The constraints imposed by looking at individual employers' responses arise from the tendency to generalize from a few examples to the universe of employers when the examples are not a statistically valid or reliable sample of the field.[10]

To create a statistically reliable sample, a researcher can call all the employers of a particular job title in an area (a census) where the employer universe is small and identifiable. Alternatively, when the potential employer base is too large to explore completely, the researcher can pick a random set from a larger number, such as every fourth or tenth listing. (This description of random sampling is highly simplified.) Labor market researchers rarely if ever use standard statistical methods to reach the universe of potentially suitable employers to contact directly for information about a job title. Their outreach to the employer base may be scattered but cannot be defined as a statistically random method. When making telephone or email contact with employers, recruiters, or staffing agencies, labor market researchers do not apply statistical approaches in determining whom to call.

For example, a researcher can probably call all or most of the ski resorts in a defined resort area to ask about the availability of jobs for ski lift operators. This would create a complete census of employment opportunity in the area for this job title. The researchers probably cannot find all the employers of people who drive snowplows, however, so the calls could yield a sampling of potential employers.

In employer sampling, researchers initiate calls and emails and cite the feedback information received. The response pattern is skewed by the ease of making the contact, whether the employer representative responds to an inquiry, whether the employer is visible by having a website or a phone listing at the time of the search, or by other research biases in finding and selecting employers, and by unknown biases in the employer base. It is not possible to know whether the responses received reflect the practices of the employer base as a whole using this method, although repetition of similar information reinforces the likelihood that the information is reliable. For instance, if five of five contacts indicate a tight labor market with many candidates for a single opening, stiff competition with difficulty in finding a job for the majority of applicants can be a reasonable prediction.

EMPLOYER VARIABILITY

Job responsibilities and descriptions can differ significantly among employers and even commonly used job titles can reflect divergent employment circumstances.

One labor market research project for "hotel front desk clerk" generated multiple job listings that varied considerably.

- Salaries ranged from $10.50 per hour to $40,000 annually.

- Required work hours varied from standard full-time Monday-through-Friday daytime schedules, to shift work mostly for nights and weekends, to flexible part-time schedules.

- Employer's requirements for computer use ranged from none to skilled use of general office and proprietary software.

- Physical demands varied from prolonged standing, to sitting full-time, to walking and cleaning.

- Required knowledge and skills spanned managing constant face-to-face people contact to using computerized phone systems, to bookkeeping and handling cash and credit.

- Even job titles differed: clerk, receptionist, associate, host, agent, attendant, representative, and administrative coordinator.

Using a nonrandom approach to exploring employer's job requirements demands expert judgment about the applicability of each listing to the individual evaluee and about how frequently the employer's requirements reflect the industry's standard practices.

SOURCES OF EMPLOYER SAMPLING INFORMATION

The reliability of the information from talks with an employer representative depends on the knowledge of the contact. A telephone call to an employer may reach an assistant or a manager, a new employee or a well-informed one. A conversation with the president of a trade organization may yield detailed insider knowledge based on long-term experience and recent exposure to occupational trends; a phone call that reaches a new employee can be significantly less rewarding.

Other potential sources of community job information in addition to employers include local chapters of trade organizations and their officers, human resource departments, staffing agencies and recruiters, professional and licensing groups, authors of articles in scholarly journals, magazines, or trade/professional journals or newspapers.

Recruiters' information may be current but if the recruiter does not specialize in the right job area, level of responsibility, or geography, his or her feedback may be less applicable to the evaluee's situation.

TIMING

The ability to make accurate predictions of future job availability may depend on the timing of the search for employer information. Seasonality of employment demand is common in many industries: teaching, retail sales, tax accounting, hospitality and tourism, and construction are examples of jobs with seasonal fluctuations in hiring and job availability.

Seasonal hiring is influenced by recurring annual events such as the school year or holidays, common schedules for travel and business conferences, or unpredictable events such as weather, consumer behavior fluctuations, and economic changes such as booms, recessions, and funding cycles.

Searching for jobs for ski instructors is difficult, if not impossible, in June; predicting teacher hiring in March before school budgets are known or legislative mandates are enacted is less accurate than it would be in August. Hiring in retail sales is easier to assess in the fourth quarter of the year. For tax accountants the same holds true in the first quarter of the year or even late in the fourth quarter.

INFORMATION AVAILABILITY

Employers fill the majority of job openings through the unadvertised, or hidden, job market. (Jones, 2005) A common estimate is that 80 percent of the available jobs are filled through personal contacts. (Job Star, 2011) These jobs obviously represent an important portion of the labor market but their requirements, availability, incidence, salaries, and other details are not available except through anecdotal sources or employer sampling.

Detailed information about some job titles and occupations is not readily available because the positions are not broadcast openly. Some common job titles like administrative assistant are unannounced because employers find it easier, more reliable, and less expensive to hire through existing employees. In times of high unemployment, employers may try to avoid the deluge of applications from a publicly advertised job opening.

Other jobs in the hidden job market demand unique talents and/or high levels of responsibility. These often are filled without public announcements, but through recruiters or personal contacts. Examples are CEOs and some other C-level positions, professional athletes, artists, musicians, and actors. Some jobs are uniquely built around the skills offered by a known candidate and do not exist until the right candidate and opportunity coincide.

Although the general announcement of a job opening may be public, it is often impossible to gain direct access to a hiring party without insider contacts. Even when a researcher gains such access, employers are guarded in response to questions about qualifications, salaries and other compensation, and similar information.

◆◆◆

Demonstrating opportunity to work through labor market research uses multiple approaches; it demands considerable expertise and judgment from the vocational evaluator to result in competent evidence for the court and attorneys.

CHAPTER NINE – MOTIVATION AND COOPERATION

When work is a pleasure, life is a joy! When work is duty, life is slavery.

Maxim Gorky

I don't want to be here. My husband and his attorney sent me, or maybe it was the court. I think my attorney okayed it, so I'm here, but I don't think it's fair to give me more to do while I'm dealing with all of the divorce paperwork and everything else. I'm just so overwhelmed, work is the last thing I want to think about. My husband doesn't want to support me so he's going to get the court to force me to go to work.

LEGAL BASIS FOR CONSIDERING MOTIVATION AND COOPERATION

The courts in California assume that any parent who is capable of working has the willingness to work. Once known as the "third prong" of the test for earning capacity,[11] the court eliminated *willingness to work* as an evaluated factor, as it should be taken for granted. (Reminder: the other two prongs are *ability to work* and *opportunity to work*.)

Richmond orders (Richmond (CA 1980) establish the expectation that a spouse should "exercise reasonable diligence" in preparing to be self-supporting, such as following a vocational plan and seeking work.

In Berland (CA 1989), the court confirmed its need to stay involved in determining support while it takes into account the supported spouse's obligation to exercise reasonable diligence to become self-supporting. Actions toward employment are manifestations of reasonable diligence that demonstrate the motivation and cooperation spouses are assumed to have. Showing diligence, or lack of it, in becoming self-supporting can influence the court's decisions about support.

In family law cases where motivation to earn was questioned, the courts have clarified what is a good reason for lowered income. In the case of Pencovic (CA 1955), the father went into the "religious guru business." The State Supreme Court held that "he had the earning capacity" to pay the support he was ordered to pay. He could not "evade" his obligation by "refusing for religious reasons to seek or accept gainful employment."

Several other cases have affirmed a court's ability to consider motivation as manifest in the spouse's behavior to modify the amount or duration of spousal support. The Sheridan court (CA 1983) said a change in support was warranted if "the supported spouse has failed to diligently seek employment sufficient to become self-supporting" or "had done little to prepare herself for or to seek gainful employment." Similarly in Rosan (CA 1972), the court can change support if the supported party "has unreasonably delayed or refused to seek employment consistent with her or his ability." The Sheridan court also found that there is no requirement to find that the failure to exercise diligence in seeking gainful employment has been in bad faith. The courts have addressed the issue of willingness, or motivation, multiple times. In Shaffer (CA 1999), the court explained that, "a supported spouse cannot make unwise [employment] decisions which have the effect of preventing him or her from becoming self-supporting and expect the supporting spouse to pick up the tab."

While the courts have repeatedly asserted that ex-spouses and parents are assumed to have the responsibility, and thus the motivation, to work, they consider the practicality of many influences in determining the reasonable earning capacity, not just the maximum possible income he or she has earned or could earn.

Vocational evaluations are especially effective in informing the court about the diligence of efforts to find work and assessing the individual's reasonable earning capacity. Vocational evaluators do not measure malingering or attribute motivations to the evaluee. They report on behaviors and consider whether the behaviors demonstrate adequate compliance, or not, with the expected efforts to search for work and achieve earnings. With their experience in seeing many job seekers and their expertise about employment and hiring, vocational evaluators can compare effective job search methods with the demonstrated search activities reported by the evaluee. See Chapter 5 regarding evaluees who are job seeking.

IMPUTED INCOME

Participants in litigation recognize that even a job seeker with wanted skills can sabotage a job interview if he or she does not want a job offer to result. The court can order the person to seek work and is especially inclined to compel the parent to find work if there is a question of sufficient income to pay child support. California Family Code Section 3558 (See Appendix D) states:

> *In a proceeding involving child or family support, a court may require either parent to attend job training, job placement and vocational rehabilitation, and work programs, as designated by the court, at regular intervals and times and for durations specified by the court, and provide documentation of participation in the programs, in a format that is acceptable to the court, in order to enable the court to make a finding that good faith attempts at job training and placement have been undertaken by the parent.*

The courts have created the method to circumvent a person's refusal to seek or accept work by imposing the financial responsibility for income production whether or not the evaluee is working. The imputation of income—assigning an amount of income a person is capable of earning—is this allocation of responsibility. The amount of imputed income connected to earning capacity can be calculated using data from a vocational evaluation.

California courts have long asserted the power to impute income to supporting spouses and parents based on ability to earn income, as distinct from actual income.

North Carolina family law defines imputed or potential income as what a parent reasonably could be expected to receive from employment or other sources if she or he took reasonable steps to do so, especially in the matter of child support. The North Carolina courts attend to the issue of motivation when imputing income, noting the difference between actual and potential income when the "parent's bad faith" reflects a "deliberate disregard" of his or her financial responsibility to support a child. The NC courts do not impute potential income to a supporting parent unless there is evidence of bad faith in these or other forms: (1) failing to exercise his reasonable capacity to earn, (2) deliberately avoiding his family's financial responsibilities, (3) acting in deliberate disregard for his support obligations, (4) refusing to seek or to accept gainful employment, (5) willfully [sic] refusing to secure or take a job, (6) deliberately not applying himself to his business, (7) intentionally depressing his income to an artificial low, or (8) intentionally leaving his employment to go into another business. (Saxon, 2008)

In vocational evaluations, the evaluator can explain the concept of imputed income and discuss applicable state law with the evaluee. With the assumption that each party will make a good faith effort toward her or his self-support, the court does not have to "make" someone "go to work." If spouses decide that they do not want to work, they carry the financial responsibility for that decision by receiving less spousal or family support. The court imputes income and calculates support; they decide whether they can live on the lowered amount and whether it is worth it to them not to work. In the case of child support, especially if the family income is low enough that a child may suffer if a responsible parent does not bring in income, the court may issue a "Seek Work Order." See Appendix G for a sample form on which to report job search efforts in response to a Seek Work Order from a court.

ADDRESSING LACK OF MOTIVATION

Fear is perhaps the most common response to all the changes in a divorce – the changes in relationships, the financial picture, location, housing, and emotional connections. What may manifest as noncooperation may stem from evaluees' feelings of uncertainty, fear, insecurity, and mistrust. If the evaluator addresses these feelings directly and empathetically, the evaluee's cooperation with the evaluation can improve dramatically.

The most commonly expressed emotions about work, earnings, and the vocational evaluation may sound like these:

If I go back to work and lose my job, they are still going to expect me to be earning money and my support won't go up even if I'm not working. I'm afraid to even get a job.

What if I get fired or lose my job? They're going to blame me and say I did it on purpose so I can ask for more support.

What if I get a job and I hate it and I can't afford to leave it because my support is based on my earning steadily? I'll be stuck in a job I can't stand.

What if my kids get sick and I need to stay home, or I want to go to see them in a game? A boss isn't going to let me do that, especially if I'm new on the job.

What if I can't earn enough to afford a place large enough for the kids to have space? They're going to hate coming to stay with me.

What if I can't finish my classes in the time frame we set up? They'll want me to start working but I won't be qualified yet to get hired.

Talking openly about these feelings allows the evaluee to bring them back to the attorney and ask that they be taken into consideration in the settlement negotiations. The evaluator can discuss how to handle the return to work adjustment and possibly suggest some incentive structures in the settlement.

For instance, the settlement can allow for delays in education due to the lack of available classes or illness. The settlement can structure the support with payments that do not decrease during a fixed period at the beginning of work, giving the evaluee incentive to find work sooner.

◆◆◆

Courts avoid the impossible task of managing a person's emotional responses by assuming that the divorcing party is motivated to follow the Court's mandate that he or she contribute reasonably to self-support. The assumption permits the Court to assign the financial responsibility to the wage earner whether the wages are earned or not.

The evaluator's role is not as enforcer of the mandate but counselor. Changing evaluees' behavior by helping them see where their actions will lead, giving them expert information and advice to reduce fears and indecision, and guiding them into productive activities are all vocational counseling practices that affect motivation and its manifestations.

The best work flows out of a collaborative environment.

Steven Bochco

Collaborative law, also known as collaborative divorce or collaborative practice, is an approach to marital dissolution in which the divorcing spouses are represented by attorneys who guide them through the legal steps with an express commitment to avoid going to court. The International Association of Collaborative Professionals (IACP, 2011) describes the collaborative process as a contractual commitment to follow these three key elements:

- Negotiate a mutually acceptable settlement without having courts decide issues.

- Maintain open communication and information sharing.

- Create shared solutions acknowledging the highest priorities of everyone involved.

The pledge within Collaborative Practice contains the understanding that both attorneys and other team professionals will withdraw if either party litigates. To support the team, collaborative lawyers often invite other professionals, such as coaches, child specialists, vocational professionals, and financial specialists to join. Valued characteristics of the collaborative process are openness, a strong emphasis on communication, understanding, and support, all of which help to reduce the pain and hurt of the normal divorce.

As part of the collaborative team, attorneys bring in the vocational specialist to perform many of the same functions utilized in a litigated divorce. While much of the vocational methodology remains the same in collaborative practice as in litigated or mediated divorces, there are significant differences in communication and attorney intent. In litigation, an attorney's strategy in hiring a vocational expert is often to establish findings that will favor her or his client's finances or desires, even while knowing that the vocational expert is committed to providing neutral objective conclusions based on verifiable evidence. In collaborative divorce, the vocational expert has other roles that are explicitly stated and shared by the attorneys.

DIFFERENCES IN THE VOCATIONAL PROCESS IN COLLABORATIVE LAW

The differences between the collaborative and litigation approaches to divorce extend beyond the commitment not to use the court to decide how the couple settles the divorce. The style of communication is more open, more focused on helping the spouses be effective in their contacts with each other. The point is to develop trust and to manifest the behaviors that will foster the belief that the pair can manage this transition fairly without doing further damage to the other.

These differences in the collaborative approach transform some of the activities of the vocational specialist who is functioning still as a neutral advisor, but also as a guide for the vocational issues to the four-way team (both spouses and both attorneys).

ROLE AND TERMINOLOGY DIFFERENCES IN COLLABORATIVE LAW

- The collaborative team does not call the vocational expert an *evaluator* to avoid the implication that the vocational services are imposed upon the divorcing spouse without her or his agreement. This emphasizes that the vocational planning is not being "done to" the spouse, but is "done with" the client to her or his benefit. The vocational person is the *consultant, counselor*, or *specialist*. The collaborative team avoids the term *expert* as it designates a specific legally defined role during testimony in litigation. This is not just being fussy about nomenclature. Vocabulary is both the frame of the structure and a reflection of it. Vocabulary sets the tone of the relationship, defines the role of the vocational person, and establishes expectations in the parties.

- The vocational consultant acts as an advisor to the attorneys and to the parties as a group in helping them understand the dynamics of the work issues and the implications of the earnings projections.

- The vocational consultant functions as vocational counselor to the nonworking spouse. The major difference between this activity and similar vocational counseling conducted outside of divorce is that there is no confidentiality in the process. A primary goal is to report the results of the vocational decision-making to the team.

- A vocational counselor's usual outcome in collaborative practice is to build a vocational plan, if one is possible. If it is not, the vocational consultant explains the reasons. In litigated cases, the creation of a vocational plan may or may not be a desired outcome, depending on whether the nonworking spouse wants to work and has enough income to live without working. In litigated cases, the vocational conclusions may lead to imputed income; this is not usually a goal in collaborative cases.

- In both collaborative and litigated cases, the vocational services include labor market research and identification of potential earnings associated with job alternatives. As in litigated cases, the collaborative vocational specialist projects potential earnings as clearly and realistically as possible, with the distinct intent not to favor one party or the other.

- In both collaborative and litigated cases, the vocational expert assesses important factors in the spouse's vocational choice and planning.

- At the request of the team, the vocational counselor may offer career coaching support after the settlement, which could involve counseling for vocational plan implementation, resume and cover letter writing, help in finding references, interviewing rehearsal, employer identification, and structure for the job search.

If the case falls out of the collaborative mode into mediation or litigation, it is not clear whether the vocational consultant can continue to work with the nonworking spouse to use completed vocational planning in future litigation. Often a signed agreement will state that unless the participants and the vocational counselor agree otherwise in writing, the vocational counselor will not appear as an expert witness for either party to testify as to any matter related to the work product created as part of this collaborative law process.

COMMUNICATION DIFFERENCES IN COLLABORATIVE LAW

- The parties and attorneys do not hold unilateral communication in the collaborative vocational services except for exchanges of information between the counselor and the nonworking spouse as they meet for counseling. The vocational expert always speaks or writes to both attorneys simultaneously unless there is an explicit agreement that this need not happen.

- The vocational counselor may initiate contact with any of the participants, their attorneys or other members of the collaborative team (financial specialist, coach, child specialist, physician, therapist, other) to request or convey information. Any member of the team may initiate contact with the counselor to add information pertinent to the vocational services.

- In collaborative cases, the vocational specialist often talks to the two attorneys in a precase conference to establish expectations and define what services they are requesting.

- In collaborative cases, the vocational specialist only conveys the results of the vocational services in a written document by request. If a written report is desired, it goes to both attorneys first or simultaneously to all four members of the team, in hard copy, by facsimile, email, or presented in a four- or five-way meeting.

- If written, the report focuses on vocational plan details, rather than hypothetical vocations for imputed income calculations. The report uses the terms *options, alternatives, suggestions* rather than *conclusions* or *recommendations*, to ensure that the supporting party understands that the vocational plan is not final until the team has agreed upon it. The plan worked out between the vocational counselor and the nonworking spouse is a best effort to convey what the spouse wants and how they expect him or her to reach the targeted job, but it is not a mandate to the team until all agree.

- If there is no written report, the results of the vocational services are conveyed to the team in other ways.

  - Oral communication between the vocational counselor and the spouse participant who then brings the plan back to the team.

  - Oral reporting in five-way meetings, with the non-working spouse describing her or his vocational plan, with further detail, explanation, or justification supplied by the vocational counselor as a supportive voice.

  - Oral communication in a four-way telephone conference, without the presence of the vocational counselor.

  - Oral communication in a four-way meeting.

  - Oral communication individually with all participants.

- Unless agreed otherwise, all parties hear and discuss vocational decisions and plans simultaneously.

- The vocational results are conveyed in a manner that avoids blaming and focusing on negatives, but may contain frank discussions of vocational barriers such as a lack of education or skills, time required to adjust to the world of work, or activities to build confidence and job search skills.

VOCATIONAL PROCESS DIFFERENCES IN COLLABORATIVE LAW

- In collaborative cases, vocational services do not occur without the nonworking spouse's cooperation; they are not just a labor market research based on work history to establish earnings without a personal interview.

- The vocational process may take longer because the counselor and spouse are working toward a real career decision, not just laying out options for possible later implementation. The spouse may need help in finding motivation and doing detailed and realistic planning.

- The vocational plan will always start from the client's interests, not merely from the fastest way to return to work or the way to earn the most. It may describe a longer plan to build a career and greater future earning capacity instead of focusing on immediate employment. However, the plan will always take into consideration the burden on the supporting spouse imposed by delays in earnings.

- The vocational plan may be longer because of parenting considerations such as extensions to accommodate summers and other vacations, or to help the reentry spouse ease into the work world.

- The vocational plan may have contingencies built in for extensions to accommodate barriers and anticipate difficulties in implementation. It may list more details about providing supportive elements such as tutors and childcare or cover transportation or other expenses.

◆◆◆

Vocational counselors are natural allies with the productive and effective collaborative team as it works toward a divorce settlement that is fair and builds toward a future with minimal conflict between divorcing parties

APPENDICES

APPENDIX A

VOCATIONAL EVALUATION: STANDARDS OF PRACTICE IN CALIFORNIA FAMILY LAW

Bay Area Vocational Experts (BAVE) is an organization of independent, experienced Northern California vocational evaluators who are committed to promoting the highest standards of vocational evaluation and counseling services through mutual support, education and shared resources.

Aware that there are no published standards for the vocational evaluations performed by mandate of the California Family Law Code, the members of BAVE have created a guide to ensure a consistent vocational evaluation process and provide a basis for understanding vocational evaluation services.

The standards are based on California Law, case law, the input of judges and attorneys, and the collective experience of the members of BAVE. www.bavocationalexperts.com

BAVE members are qualified to evaluate parties in family law cases according to the definition of Vocational Training Counselor in Family Law Code §4331(d) and (e).

The Standards are the exclusive product of the Bay Area Vocational Experts. Written permission must be obtained for reproduction or distribution.

VOCATIONAL EVALUATION

In a California family law proceeding in which either child and/or spousal support is requested, the earning capacity of both the payor and recipient must be considered.

The function of the Vocational Evaluation in Family Law is to provide the judges, mediators and/or judicial officers and the parties with objective, verifiable information regarding employment issues for use in determining appropriate support levels. In California, vocational evaluations may be ordered by the court, requested by one party, or agreed to by both parties.

THE ROLE OF THE VOCATIONAL EXPERT

1. To provide objective, verifiable employment information to the triers of fact and the parties, the vocational expert

    a. Evaluates relevant individual attributes related to marketable skills, which may include

        i. age

        ii. education

        iii. employment history

        iv. interests and values

        v. physical and psychological conditions or limitations

        vi. transferable employment skills and abilities

        vii. psychosocial factors, such as legal issues, secondary sources of income or special needs of dependent children

    b. Identifies potential occupations, if appropriate.

    c. Conducts current, relevant labor market research to determine earning capacity and access to employment opportunities associated with the identified occupations.

    d. Provides vocational planning, when appropriate, by outlining the steps to achieve a vocational goal, training programs, costs, reasonable timelines, and potential barriers in a vocational plan.

2. To maintain objectivity throughout the vocational evaluation process, regardless of the source of the referral, the vocational expert

    a. Receives and evaluates information relevant to the vocational evaluation.

    b. Makes reasonable effort to obtain relevant information needed to form an expert opinion.

    c. Forms expert opinions and bases conclusions on all relevant information available.

    d. Discloses the need for information that is unavailable but necessary to form an expert opinion.

3. To ensure ethical treatment of the individual being evaluated, the vocational expert

   a. Discloses to the person being evaluated the role of the independent vocational expert as evaluator and not a provider of services.

   b. Discloses the limits of confidentiality to the person being evaluated.

   c. Discloses the potential for a conclusion with which the person being evaluated may not agree.

4. To communicate with all parties consistent with the assigned role as expert, the vocational expert

Communicates with the parties according to the stated arrangements:

   a. When retained by one party, the expert communicates orally and in writing with that party solely, unless otherwise directed.

   b. When both parties jointly request the evaluation, the expert communicates orally and in writing with both parties simultaneously. The expert requires written information offered by either party to be provided simultaneously to the other party.

   c. When appointed as the court's expert according to Evidence Code §730, the expert may contact or request information from either party or attorney directly, or request a joint conference. Neither party may initiate contact with the expert without prior agreement. Neither party may submit written material to the expert without simultaneously submitting a copy to the other party. The expert submits written reports simultaneously to the court and to both attorneys/parties.

THE RESPONSIBILITIES OF THE VOCATIONAL EXPERT

5. To gather relevant information relevant to the person being evaluated that is necessary to complete the evaluation, the vocational expert

Follows a standardized vocational evaluation process which may include

   a. Diagnostic interview.

   b. Vocational testing.

   c. Review of vocational test results with person being evaluated.

   d. Other relevant information specific to the case.

6. To provide for informed participation in the vocational evaluation, the vocational exper.t

a. Considers the issues of diversity including age, gender, sexual orientation, religion, country of origin, disability, language ability, ethnicity and cultural difference.

b. Explains the influence of individual's motivation and cooperation and the possible consequences on the evaluation.

c. Explains the option of using the evaluation findings and vocational plan for the individual's personal career planning.

d. Explains the concept of imputed income that can be determined through the evaluation findings.

e. Requests the cooperation of the person being evaluated in providing needed information and integrates the individual's feedback in the evaluation.

7. To gather relevant labor market information, the vocational expert

a. Determines the appropriate sources of information about salaries, wages and job availability.

b. Conducts research appropriate to the occupation, geographic location, and individual attributes of the person being evaluated.

c. Provides current accurate information relevant to the occupations.

d. Weighs the labor market information on the basis of its source, currency, and applicability.

THE VOCATIONAL EVALUATION REPORT

8. To report the vocational opinions, conclusions and recommendations, the vocational expert

a. Determines the ability of the person being evaluated to engage in paid employment.

b. Identifies the factors influencing vocational outcomes.

c. Identifies alternative vocational objectives.

d. Identifies the need for retraining or education to acquire marketable skills and/or employment for each objective. The expert provides a description of the training costs and duration.

e. Details salary and other earning information and job availability associated with the vocational objectives.

f. Includes sources and methods of collection of labor market and other information

g. Evaluates the good faith efforts of the person being evaluated to maximize self-support.

h. Recommends a vocational plan, taking into consideration the marital standard of living and the goal that the supported party shall be self-supporting within a reasonable period of time.

i. Recommends steps to implement the vocational plan.

j. Provides a written report, as ordered or requested.

k. Provides testimony on the vocational evaluation process, conclusions and opinions at the request of the attorney(s) or the court.

APPENDIX B

CALIFORNIA FAMILY CODE SECTIONS 4320-4322

Division 9 Support
Part 3 Spousal Support

4320. In ordering spousal support under this part, the court shall consider all of the following circumstances:

(a) The extent to which the earning capacity of each party is sufficient to maintain the standard of living established during the marriage, taking into account all of the following:

(1) The marketable skills of the supported party; the job market for those skills; the time and expenses required for the supported party to acquire the appropriate education or training to develop those skills; and the possible need for retraining or education to acquire other, more marketable skills or employment.

(2) The extent to which the supported party's present or future earning capacity is impaired by periods of unemployment that were incurred during the marriage to permit the supported party to devote time to domestic duties.

(b) The extent to which the supported party contributed to the attainment of an education, training, a career position, or a license by the supporting party.

(c) The ability of the supporting party to pay spousal support, taking into account the supporting party's earning capacity, earned and unearned income, assets, and standard of living.

(d) The needs of each party based on the standard of living established during the marriage.

(e) The obligations and assets, including the separate property, of each party.

(f) The duration of the marriage.

(g) The ability of the supported party to engage in gainful employment without unduly interfering with the interests of dependent children in the custody of the party.

(h) The age and health of the parties.

(i) Documented evidence of any history of domestic violence, as defined in Section 6211, between the parties, including, but not limited to, consideration of emotional distress resulting from domestic violence perpetrated against the supported party by the supporting party, and consideration of any history of violence against the supporting party by the supported party.

(j) The immediate and specific tax consequences to each party.

(k) The balance of the hardships to each party.

(l) The goal that the supported party shall be self-supporting within a reasonable period of time. Except in the case of a marriage of long duration as described in Section 4336, a "reasonable period of time" for purposes of this section generally shall be one-half the length of the marriage. However, nothing in this section is intended to limit the court's discretion to order support for a greater or lesser length of time, based on any of the other factors listed in this section, Section 4336, and the circumstances of the parties.

(m) The criminal conviction of an abusive spouse shall be considered in making a reduction or elimination of a spousal support award in accordance with Section 4325.

(n) Any other factors the court determines are just and equitable.

4321. In a judgment of dissolution of marriage or legal separation of the parties, the court may deny support to a party out of the separate property of the other party in any of the following circumstances:

(a) The party has separate property, or is earning the party's own livelihood, or there is community property or quasi-community property sufficient to give the party proper support.

(b) The custody of the children has been awarded to the other party, who is supporting them.

4322. In an original or modification proceeding, where there are no children, and a party has or acquires a separate estate, including income from employment, sufficient for the party's proper support, no support shall be ordered or continued against the other party.

Appendices

APPENDIX C

CALIFORNIA FAMILY CODE SECTIONS 4330-4331

Division 9 Support
Part 3 Spousal Support

4330. (a) In a judgment of dissolution of marriage or legal separation of the parties, the court may order a party to pay for the support of the other party an amount, for a period of time, that the court determines is just and reasonable, based on the standard of living established during the marriage, taking into consideration the circumstances as provided in Chapter 2 (commencing with Section 4320).

(b) When making an order for spousal support, the court may advise the recipient of support that he or she should make reasonable efforts to assist in providing for his or her support needs, taking into account the particular circumstances considered by the court pursuant to Section 4320, unless, in the case of a marriage of long duration as provided for in Section 4336, the court decides this warning is inadvisable.

4331. (a) In a proceeding for dissolution of marriage or for legal separation of the parties, the court may order a party to submit to an examination by a vocational training counselor. The examination shall include an assessment of the party's ability to obtain employment based upon the party's age, health, education, marketable skills, employment history, and the current availability of employment opportunities. The focus of the examination shall be on an assessment of the party's ability to obtain employment that would allow the party to maintain herself or himself at the marital standard of living.

(b) The order may be made only on motion, for good cause, and on notice to the party to be examined and to all parties. The order shall specify the time, place, manner, conditions, scope of the examination, and the person or persons by whom it is to be made.

(c) A party who does not comply with an order under this section is subject to the same consequences provided for failure to comply with an examination ordered pursuant to Section 2032 of the Code of Civil Procedure.

(d) "Vocational training counselor" for the purpose of this section means an individual with sufficient knowledge, skill, experience, training, or education in interviewing, administering, and interpreting tests for analysis of marketable skills, formulating career goals, planning courses of training and study, and assessing the job market, to qualify as an expert in vocational training under Section 720 of the Evidence Code.

(e) A vocational training counselor shall have at least the following qualifications:

(1) A master's degree in the behavioral sciences.

(2) Be qualified to administer and interpret inventories for assessing career potential.

(3) Demonstrated ability in interviewing clients and assessing marketable skills with understanding of age constraints, physical and mental health, previous education and experience, and time and geographic mobility constraints.

(4) Knowledge of current employment conditions, job market, and wages in the indicated geographic area.

(5) Knowledge of education and training programs in the area with costs and time plans for these programs.

(f) The court may order the supporting spouse to pay, in addition to spousal support, the necessary expenses and costs of the counseling, retraining, or education.

APPENDIX D

CALIFORNIA FAMILY CODE SECTIONS 3558, 4058

<u>Division 9. Support</u>
<u>Part 1. Definitions And General Provisions</u>

3558. In a proceeding involving child or family support, a court may require either parent to attend job training, job placement and vocational rehabilitation, and work programs, as designated by the court, at regular intervals and times and for durations specified by the court, and provide documentation of participation in the programs, in a format that is acceptable to the court, in order to enable the court to make a finding that good faith attempts at job training and placement have been undertaken by the parent.

<u>Division 9. Support</u>
<u>Part 2. Child Support</u>
<u>Chapter 2. Court-Ordered Child Support</u>
<u>Article 2. Statewide Uniform Guideline</u>

4058. (a) The annual gross income of each parent means income from whatever source derived . . . includes, but is not limited to, the following:

(3) In the discretion of the court, employee benefits or self-employment benefits, taking into consideration the benefit to the employee, any corresponding reduction in living expenses, and other relevant facts.

(b) The court may, in its discretion, consider the earning capacity of a parent in lieu of the parent's income, consistent with the best interests of the children.

APPENDIX E

CALIFORNIA EVIDENCE CODE SECTION 730

When it appears to the court, at any time before or during the trial of an action, that expert evidence is or may be required by the court or by any party to the action, the court on its own motion or on motion of any party may appoint one or more experts to investigate, to render a report as may be ordered by the court, and to testify as an expert at the trial of the action relative to the fact or matter as to which the expert evidence is or may be required.

The court may fix the compensation for these services, if any, rendered by any person appointed under this section, in addition to any service as a witness, at the amount as seems reasonable to the court.

Nothing in this section shall be construed to permit a person to perform any act for which a license is required unless the person holds the appropriate license to lawfully perform that act.

Last modified: March 8, 2010

APPENDIX F

THE DISCLOSURE FORM

Note: this form is part of the discussion in the initial interview with the evaluee. The words "you" and "your" refer to the evaluee; the words "I", "me," and "my" refer to the vocational evaluator. The vocational evaluator signs the form at the bottom to indicate that the discussion has taken place. The original remains in the evaluator's file; a copy is given to the evaluee.

Vocational Evaluation Disclosure Statement

You have been referred by

_____

to receive a vocational evaluation. The purpose of this evaluation is to assess your ability to work. I will be providing an opinion regarding appropriate alternate employment, your earning capacity, return to work barriers, and recommendations to overcome such, if possible.

My Role and Responsibilities

I have been retained to provide an opinion only and I have not been retained to provide any services that I might recommend to expedite your return to work. I may be asked to testify in a legal proceeding regarding information obtained during your assessment and my opinion regarding your employability, earning capacity, and recommendations for dealing with any identified employment barriers. I may be asked to write a report about my findings and opinions. I may need to communicate with attorneys, medical professionals or other sources of information to develop information and form conclusions. Services may include vocational interviews, testing and interpretation when appropriate, collection of relevant data, labor market research, reporting, testifying, and communicating with the parties and attorneys or other information sources needed to form a professional opinion.

Your Role and Responsibilities

Your role is to provide accurate information in response to my questions. If you do not understand the reason for a particular question that I may ask, you have the right to request an explanation before responding. You may be asked to follow through with assignments. If you do not understand or do not wish to perform the assignments, you should let me know.

Benefits to You

A benefit to you of undergoing this process is that I will provide an objective and unbiased opinion regarding your vocational options, employability, earning capacity, and barriers to employment. You will be able to ask questions, and I will do my best to answer them for you. You may find the vocational recommendations helpful.

Lack of Confidentiality

This evaluation is taking place within the context of legal action. It is important that you understand that any information that I receive from you or other sources during the course of this evaluation and formulation of my opinion is not confidential and could be shared in my report or in a legal proceeding. I may involve other professionals to assist me with various aspects of developing my opinion. Discussions regarding your case may be held with such individuals. Depending upon the referral source, I may or may not be providing a written report. Your attorney will be provided with a copy of my report if one is issued. The normal confidentiality considerations of a client-counselor relationship do not apply in this context.

Records and Electronic Communication

[Vocational Evaluator name] will keep the case file for the duration of the case, or for two years following the conclusion of the legal matter if this date is known. Some information may be conveyed electronically. Reasonable efforts to ensure that electronically conveyed information via fax or email is available only to the appropriate addressees will be made. Some risk may be associated with electronic communication. Records will be released only to referring parties, those authorized by referring parties, and in response to a subpoena.

Besides the above-noted limits on confidentiality, these additional situations may require that I divulge information concerning you:

- If I believe that you are going to harm or endanger yourself or others, I am required to notify the endangered individual(s), the proper authorities and/or officials.

- If I believe you are going to harm or endanger or abuse children or the elderly, I must report this to state or local authorities.

- Requests for information from other parties (i.e. doctors, physical therapists, your employer, etc.) involved in your case may occur. If so, you will be asked to sign a release of information form so your records can be released. That signature is voluntary.

- If a properly issued subpoena is received in the context of a lawsuit or other legal proceeding, then information in your file may be released.

- If you are a minor or *not* your own legal guardian, then the information in your file may be available to your legal guardian or advocate.

Risks to You

There may be some risks involved in the vocational assessment process. My opinion will be arrived at objectively and you may not agree with my opinion or feel that it is not favorable to your case. I will be glad to discuss my opinions with you.

Appendices

Qualifications and Sources of Further Information

I have a Bachelor's degree in [*fill in*] and a Master's degree in [*fill in*]. I have been conducting evaluations since [*fill in*]. I am a [*fill in qualifications and certifications*] and am a member of [*fill in professional organizations*]. You may request a copy of my resume and professional qualifications. Should you have any concerns, please contact me or the professional organizations to which I belong.

Acknowledgment

I will review the following topics with you and sign this form to note that this has been done. You will be given a copy of the form but do not need to sign it.

- My roles and responsibilities

- Limitations on what I can do

- Your roles and responsibilities

- Confidentiality

- Frequency and length of service

- Nature and type of rehabilitation services provided

- Risks and benefits involved with vocational rehabilitation services

- Risks associated with electronic communication

- Potential of my providing testimony in a court setting regarding your case

- Records preservation

I attest that I have discussed the aforementioned topics with the evaluee.

_____   _____
Signature of Counselor   Date

_____
Printed Name of Evaluee

APPENDIX G

SEEK WORK ORDER FORM

Use this form to report to the Court about weekly efforts made to find work.

Weekly Job Search Log					
Name				Week of:	
Date	Activity*	Contact/ Organization	Results	Follow-up Steps (what you are going to do & when)	Time spent (start & end time)

Page _____ of _____

* Activities to report include: networking contacts; informational and job interviews; follow up with prior contacts; finding and responding to ads for job openings; online research about companies, industries and jobs; job search skill training; job club participation; job coaching appointments; trade, union, or professional organization contacts; contacts with alumni groups and placement agencies; writing and submitting resumes and cover letters; other job-related communication.

APPENDIX H

JOB SEARCH GUIDELINES

To be effective, Job Search is an organized process, at least 20-30 hours per week, using 2-5 methods of <u>active</u> job contacts.

<u>Examples of active job search</u> – calling, sending resumes to specific employers, speaking to people in person, sending emails.

<u>Examples of passive job search</u> – reading job want ads, researching jobs online, reading journal articles, posting resumes on general job websites

John Challenger, President of the nationally-known outplacement firm Challenger, Gray & Christmas says, *"Simply posting resumes on Internet job sites and answering classified ads **rarely work, even in a good job market**. These activities are even less effective in a weak job market."*

Networking is the most effective strategy for finding employment. The Wall Street Journal reported (Sarah Needleman, *Internal Hires, Referrals Most Hired in 2009*, 2/19/10) that more than half (51%) of employers' job openings were filled by promotions and internal transfers in 2009. More than half (27%) of the remaining 49% of the open jobs filled by applicants from outside the company were found through referrals. Companies hired one person for every 15 referrals. They hired 22% from their own web sites and 13% from other job boards.

From a poll of Silicon Valley jobseekers in 2011, 52% found their current jobs through personal referrals (networking), 16% through contacting the employer directly 15% through recruiters, 15% through want ads, and 2% through social networking online.

Discussing how executives find work, the *2010 Executive Job Market Intelligence Report* from ExecuNet states, ***"Networking, both online and off, is the primary success activity for job seekers to create or identify career options*.**" About 90% of $200k+ positions are not openly posted. Hiring managers turn to their networks of colleagues and peers for referrals and shy away from advertising openings to avoid the volume of applicants. Executives find jobs by networking (68%), responding to job postings (13%), research to identify companies and potential contacts (8%), posting resumes in online databases (4%), and maintaining an online profile to attract contacts (4%).

Appendices

Prepare to Job Search

Resume, Cover Letters, Interview Answers

- You must have an email address. Make sure it is professional sounding. You can create an email just for job search. You may not want to use your home address on your resume, but you will always need to list an email address and phone number.

- Write a basic resume and cover letter drafts.

- Edit the resume and cover letter for each job type you will apply for.

- Customize your resume and cover letter to match specific job listings.

- If you submit your application as an email attachment, your email will be used as a cover letter. Write it as a cover letter, not as an informal note.

- Covers letters are not read as often as resumes and may be ignored by large companies, but a poorly written cover letter can eliminate you from employer consideration.

- If your resumes are not getting responses, have someone respected in the field review it for errors, active language, achievement statements, clear goals and related skills

- Learn how to write a resume that works for online hiring to get through the applicant tracking systems (ATS) that reaches HR screeners and keyword search engines. Use the employer's vocabulary, jargon, and wording contained in the job descriptions or want ads.

- If you use a summary list of qualifications at the top of the resume, list your key functional and technical skills, not your personal qualities.

- Craft a 10-second, 30-second, and 60-second pitch. Each pitch must explain why you are looking for a job, what you are looking for, and offer proof you are good at the job.

- Have a ready answer for the questions that you will be asked most often. For example, "What have you been doing since you worked last?"

- Read interview advice and practice interviewing.

References and Online Presence

- Collect 3-5 references, then list them on a separate page with the same header as your resume. Speak to your references about what you would like discussed if they are called.

- Utilize appropriate internet social networking sites, such as LinkedIn or Facebook, targeted toward your career goal. Be careful what you say about yourself and do not concentrate on social networking as your only job search method.

- Research how you will appear to potential employers by Googling yourself and tracing your online reputation.

- If appropriate, build a website to show your portfolio or start a focused blog about professional concerns.

- Use appropriate social media for your professional profile.

Networking Preparation

- Keep or create an extensive list of personal and professional network contacts, former colleagues, teachers, mentors, associates.

- Contact your college's alumni support services and network of graduates.

- Research technological, procedural and legislative changes in the market.

- Conduct informational interviews with business contacts to help gather information and renew a contact list.

- Consider having a business card which lists your name, key skills, email and phone number as a handy tool to give to people you meet especially, when a resume isn't appropriate.

Temporary Work or Consulting

- If you take free lance or temporary consulting jobs to fill in until you have a full time job, make sure that they are worth your time and do not interfere with your job search. To decide whether or not to take a consulting job, ask yourself these questions:

  - Does it leave me time for my job search?

  - Would I learn anything new?

  - Does the firm have a reputation that adds to mine?

  - Will I be isolated or in contact with people to add to my network?

  - Does it demand travel that will interfere with my job search?

  - Is the compensation worth my time?

Make Active Contacts

Online Research

- Use online research to find people with whom to make personal contact.

- Identify 25 employers at a time you would like to work for, without regard to whether they are currently advertising any openings.

- Research the 25 employers. Simply look at the company website and Google the employer's name. Have a file in which you stores notes about each employer.

- Visit each of the 25 employers' websites and apply for any appropriate jobs. Apply for listed jobs or write a brief email to the Chief Executive Officer (CEO) or other senior employee.

- Research the company for a Facebook page or a LinkedIn job announcement.

- Read the website and other online company information to look for more than just job openings. From a website, you can learn more about the company, the industry, and individuals.

- Use employer websites to learn the vocabulary used to describe skills so you can use these key words on your resume.

- Note the licenses, certifications, degrees and other credentials held by experienced members of the field; use job announcements to see which are requested most frequently.

- Find the trade organizations the company belongs to. Then research other members of those trade organizations to find more potential employers. Join the local chapter of the trade organization. Call the local chapter officers for informational interviews.

- Identify trade journals to read to keep up with industry trends and hiring practices.

- Note the names of managers, department heads, and major industry leaders. Read their resumes to find out what training they had, their career steps, their licenses and certifications.

Personal Contacts

- Contact the 25 people in your network most likely to help you get a job, using email, in-person conversations, or phone. Tell your contacts what two to three skills make you qualified. Ask for leads and follow up on their suggestions.

- Continue making personal contacts with the next 25, and the next, and with the new referrals received from other search activity.

- If you have not heard from people you have contacted, call to follow up by email or voice mail.

- Write thank you notes or emails to anyone who has helped you.

Recruiters

- Build relationships with search or temporary or permanent staffing firms.

- If you are new to a field, a recruiter will not be able to help place you in a job, but may be able to tell you how to make contacts.

- There are two types of recruiters, distinguished by how they are paid. Contingency recruiters fill jobs paying less than $100K+ salaries, often filling multiple vacancies with similar candidates. Retained recruiters are often used to find unique or specialized candidates and to pre-screen and interview candidates for jobs paying $100K+ salaries.

- Make calls to recruiters without relying on them to provide placement but more to provide industry information. Recruiters are often highly specialized; find one that works in your specific industry and role.

- Use recruiters to find out what skills employers value most and whether you would be a good candidate.

Trade Organizations

- Volunteer in a professional or trade organization to establish trusted relationships

- Use local contacts in a trade organization for informational interviewing

- Attend professional organization monthly meetings, special events and conferences

- Use trade organization membership lists to identify potential employers.

Schools

- Use the placement offices and job boards for any school to which you have access

- Talk to former instructors and department heads for referrals for job leads, informational interviews and suggestions for appropriate job titles and employers

- Apply for internships or externships for experience and references

Job Search Assistance

- You may want to work with a career coach to help support and structure your efforts.

- Participate in workshops and seminars about resume writing, interviewing and job finding at local EDD offices or other community support services.

Keep Records

Documentation

- Keep daily records of hours spent, contacts made and follow up details.

- Keep a database of contacts and activities

- Track websites seen, jobs applied for, types of responses, re-contact dates

General Job Search websites

Use these sites to

- Identify job titles for jobs you might like to do

- See what qualifications employers want

- Identify employers and types of employers to search

- Find trade organizations to explore

- Get a sense of salary levels

- Explore what jobs are advertised openly

- Put quotes around job titles you are looking for to narrow your search to your exact specifications.

Don't – Don't – Don't

- DON'T use the sites as the only way you search for jobs. Networking works better.

- DON'T think that the only jobs available are those you see listed online. Most jobs, perhaps 80% of all jobs that get filled, are never posted publicly.

- DON'T substitute the preparation and documentation activities (I and III) for making active contacts (II). Though job search preparation and documentation are important, they will not create job offers.

- Use some of the following as websites to get started in your research.

- ☐ 211.org for community resource
- ☐ 6FigureJobs.com
- ☐ AllHealthcareJobs.com
- ☐ CareerBuilder.com
- ☐ Craigslist.com
- ☐ Dice.com
- ☐ DirectEmployers.com
- ☐ DiversityJobs.com
- ☐ EmploymentGuide.com
- ☐ Execunet.com
- ☐ GetTheJob.com
- ☐ GOJobs.com
- ☐ Hcareers.com
- ☐ HealthCareerWeb.com
- ☐ Healthjobsusa.com
- ☐ HigherEdJobs.com
- ☐ Idealist.org
- ☐ Indeed.com

- ☐ Job.com
- ☐ JobCentral.com
- ☐ JobCircle.com
- ☐ Jobstar.com
- ☐ JobFox.com
- ☐ Jobing.com
- ☐ Juju job-search-engine.com
- ☐ Monster.com
- ☐ Net-Temps.com
- ☐ Nonprofitjobs.com
- ☐ Opportunityknocks.com
- ☐ SimplyHired.com
- ☐ SnagAJob.com
- ☐ TheLadders.com
- ☐ TopUSAJobs.com
- ☐ Universe.jobs
- ☐ Vault.com
- ☐ Yahoo! HotJobs.com

PHYSICAL FUNCTIONAL CAPACITIES FORM

A. Endurance Factors

Patient is able to	Not at All	Occasionally[1]	Frequently[2]	Continuously[3]
Be at work	_____	_____	_____	_____
Work every day	_____	_____	_____	_____
Work overtime	_____	_____	_____	_____
Stand	_____	_____	_____	_____
Walk	_____	_____	_____	_____
Sit	_____	_____	_____	_____
Drive/Ride	_____	_____	_____	_____

Note. [1] 10-33%, Up to 2.5 hrs; [2] 34-66%, 2.5 to 5 hrs; [3] 67-100%, 5 to 7.5 hrs

Patient is able to	Longest period of time	Length of breaks	How many periods/day
Stand	_____	_____	_____
Walk	_____	_____	_____
Sit	_____	_____	_____
Drive/Ride	_____	_____	_____

B. Strength Factors

Patient is able to	Not at All	Occasionally[1]	Frequently[2]	Continuously[3]
Push	_____	_____	_____	_____
Pull	_____	_____	_____	_____
Lift	_____	_____	_____	_____
Carry	_____	_____	_____	_____

Note. [1] 10-33%, Up to 2.5 hrs; [2] 34-66%, 2.5 to 5 hrs; [3] 67-100%, 5 to 7.5 hrs

Patient is able to	Heaviest weight	Distance	Frequency /day
Push	_____	_____	_____
Pull	_____	_____	_____
Lift	_____	_____	_____
Carry	_____	_____	_____

C. Physical Agility Factors

Patient is able to	Not at All	Occasionally[1]	Frequently[2]	Continuously[3]
Climb	_____	_____	_____	_____
Balance	_____	_____	_____	_____

Note. [1] 10-33%, Up to 2.5 hrs; [2] 34-66%, 2.5 to 5 hrs; [3] 67-100%, 5 to 7.5 hrs

Patient is able to	Height/ # stairs	Even/uneven surfaces	On/Above ground level
Climb	_____	_____	_____
Balance	_____	_____	_____

D. Dexterity Factors

Patient is able to	Not at All	Occasionally[1]	Frequently[2]	Continuously[3]
Reach while sitting	_____	_____	_____	_____
Above shoulder level	_____	_____	_____	_____
At shoulder level	_____	_____	_____	_____
Below shoulder level	_____	_____	_____	_____
Forward reaching	_____	_____	_____	_____
Reach side to side	_____	_____	_____	_____
Reach while standing	_____	_____	_____	_____
Above shoulder level	_____	_____	_____	_____
At shoulder level	_____	_____	_____	_____
Below shoulder level	_____	_____	_____	_____
Forward reaching	_____	_____	_____	_____
Reach side to side	_____	_____	_____	_____
HAND USE L/R/both				
Keyboard use	_____	_____	_____	_____
Extension	_____	_____	_____	_____
Flexion	_____	_____	_____	_____
Cylindrical grasp (e.g., pole)	_____	_____	_____	_____
Palmar grasp (e.g., paper clip)	_____	_____	_____	_____
Lateral grasp (e.g., piece of paper)	_____	_____	_____	_____
Reach while sitting	_____	_____	_____	_____
Above shoulder level	_____	_____	_____	_____
At shoulder level	_____	_____	_____	_____
Below shoulder level	_____	_____	_____	_____
Forward reaching	_____	_____	_____	_____
Reach side to side	_____	_____	_____	_____
Power grip	_____	_____	_____	_____
Fine manipulation	_____	_____	_____	_____
Hold steering wheel	_____	_____	_____	_____

Note. [1] 10-33%, Up to 2.5 hrs; [2] 34-66%, 2.5 to 5 hrs; [3] 67-100%, 5 to 7.5 hrs

E . Sensory Factors

Patient has restrictions	Minimal	Moderate	Acute
Hear L/R	_____	_____	_____
Speak English	_____	_____	_____
See L/R	_____	_____	_____
Night/depth vision	_____	_____	_____

F. Environmental Factors

Patient is able to work	Not at All	Occasionally[1]	Frequently[2]	Continuously[3]
Inside	_____	_____	_____	_____
Outside	_____	_____	_____	_____
Heat	_____	_____	_____	_____
Cold	_____	_____	_____	_____
Noise/vibration	_____	_____	_____	_____
Arid/humid	_____	_____	_____	_____
Gases/fumes	_____	_____	_____	_____

Note. [1] 10-33%, Up to 2.5 hrs; [2] 34-66%, 2.5 to 5 hrs; [3] 67-100%, 5 to 7.5 hrs

Notes/Comments

_____   _____

Signature/Title   Date

_____   _____   _____

Address   City State Zip   Phone

APPENDIX J

MENTAL FUNCTIONAL CAPACITIES FORM

Definitions to describe the severity of psychological impairment	
None	no limitation
Mild	impairment of slight importance – does not affect ability to function in the workplace
Moderate	an impairment which affects but does not preclude ability to function
Moderately severe	an impairment which seriously affects ability to function
Severe	extreme impairment of ability to function

Questions for treating or evaluating psychiatrist, psychologist or therapist:

1. Frequency and length of contact for evaluation and/or treatment.

2. DSM-IV Multiaxial Evaluation[12]:

   a. Axis I: Clinical Syndromes

   b. Axis II: Personality and Mental Retardation

   c. Axis III: Medical Conditions

   d. Axis IV: Psychosocial and Environmental Problems

   e. Axis V: Global Assessment of Functioning

3. Identify the patient's signs and symptoms.

4. Describe the clinical findings including results of mental status examination that demonstrate the severity of the patient's mental impairment and symptoms.

5. List prescribed medications.

6. Describe any side effects of medications which may have implications for working, e.g. dizziness, drowsiness, fatigue, lethargy, stomach upset, etc.:

For Questions 7-11, use impairment ratings above.

7. Describe how often the patient's impairments or treatment would cause absence from work, on average.

8. Describe the impairment's effect on the ability to understand, remember and carry out work tasks.

   a. Remember locations and work-like procedures

   b. Understand and remember very short, simple instructions.

   c. Carry out very short, simple instructions

   d. Understand and remember detailed instructions

   e. Carry out detailed instructions

   f. Maintain attention and concentration for extended periods, i.e. 2 hours

   g. Maintain regular attendance and be punctual

   h. Sustain an ordinary routine without special supervision

   i. Deal with stress of semi-skilled and skilled work

   j. Work in coordination with or proximity to others without being unduly distracted

   k. Make simple work-related decisions

   l. Complete a normal workday or workweek without interruptions from psychologically based symptoms

   m. Perform at a consistent pace without an unreasonable number and length of rest periods

9. Describe the impairment's effect on the ability to respond appropriately to supervision, coworkers and work pressure in a work-setting.

   a. Interact appropriately with the public

   b. Ask simple questions or request assistance.

   c. Accept instructions and respond appropriately to criticism from supervisors.

d. Get along with coworkers and peers without unduly distracting them or exhibiting behavioral extremes

e. Maintain socially appropriate behavior

f. Adhere to basic standards of neatness and cleanliness.

g. Respond appropriately to changes in a routine work setting

h. Be aware of normal hazards and take appropriate precautions

i. Travel in unfamiliar places

j. Use public transportation

k. Set realistic goals or make plans independently of others

10. Indicate to what degree the following functional limitations exist as a result of the patient's mental impairments.

a. Restriction of activities of daily living

b. Difficulties in maintaining social functioning

c. Deficiencies of concentration, persistent or pace resulting in failure to complete tasks in a timely manner (in work settings or elsewhere)

d. Episodes of deterioration or decompensation in work or work-like settings which cause the individual to withdraw from that situation or to experience exacerbation of signs and symptoms (which may include deterioration of adaptive behaviors)

Signature _____

Title _____ Date _____

Address _____

City State Zip _____ Phone _____

CALIFORNIA FAMILY LAW CASE CITATIONS

In re Marriage of Berger (2009)170 Cal.App.4th 1070

In re Marriage of Berland (1989) 215 Cal.App.3d 1257, 264 Cal.Rptr. 210

In re Marriage of Cohn (1998) 65 Cal.App.4th 923, 930,76 Cal.Rptr.2d 866

In re Marriage of Destein (2001) 91 Cal.App.4th 1385, 1392

In re Marriage of Everett (1990) 220 Cal.App.3d 846

In re Marriage of Gavron (1988) 203 Cal.App.3d 705, 712

In re Marriage of Hublou (1991) 231 Cal.App.3d 956 , 282 Cal.Rptr. 695

In re Marriage of Iredale v. Cates (2004) 121 Cal.App.4th 321

In re Marriage of Magruder (2008) not reported in Cal.Rptr.3d, 2008 WL 467699 (Cal.App. 4 Dist.)

In re Marriage of Morrison (1978) 20 Cal.3d 437, at page 451-453

In re Marriage of Padilla (1995) 38 Cal.App.4th 1212

In re Marriage of Pencovic v. Pencovic (1955) 45 Cal.2d 97

In re Marriage of Regnery (1989) 214 Cal. App. 3d 1367, 263 Cal. Rptr. 243

In re *Marriage of Reynolds* (1998) 63 Cal.App.4th 1373, 74 Cal.Rptr.2d 636

In re Marriage of Richmond (1980) 105 Cal.App.3d 352 , 164 Cal.Rptr. 381

In re Marriage of Rosan (1972) 24 Cal.App.3d 885 , 896

In re Marriage of Schaffer (1999) 69 Cal.App.4th 801, 803-804

In re Marriage of Schmir (2005)134 Cal.App.4th 43 , 35 Cal.Rptr.3d 716

In re Marriage of Shaughnessy (2006) 139 Cal.App.4th 1225 , 43 Cal.Rptr.3d 642

In re Marriage of Sheridan (1983) 140 Cal.App.3d 742 , 749

In re Marriage of Simpson (1992) 4 Cal.4th 225, 234-235

In re Marriage of Smith (2001) 90 Cal.App.4th 74, 108 Cal.Rptr.2d 537

In re Marriage of Wittgrove (2004) 120 Cal.App.4th 1317

BIBLIOGRAPHY

Data Set: 2006-2008 American Community Survey 3-Year Estimates. (2006-2008). Retrieved March 1, 2012, from U.S. Census Bureau, Selected Economic Characteristics: 2006-2008: http://factfinder. census.gov

American Board of Vocational Experts. (2007, August). *ABVE Code of Ethics.* Retrieved January 2, 2011, from American Board of Vocational Experts: http://www.abve.net/Assets/ ABVE_Code_of_Ethics_2007_cover.pdf

Ames, M. (1983). *Small Business Management.* Eagan, MN: West Group.

Bellos, D. (2011). *Is that a fish in your ear? Translation and the meaning of everything.* New York: Faber & Faber.

Blackwell, T., Dillman, E., Field, T., Grimes, J., & Weed, R. (1997). *Forensic rehabilitation: A Source for vocational experts.* Athens, GA: Elliott & Fitzpatrick.

Bureau of Labor Statistics. (2008, July). *Spotlight on statistics: Older workers.* Retrieved from Current Population Survey, http://www.bls.gov/spotlight

Bureau of Labor Statistics. (2010, March). Record unemployment among older workers does not keep them out of the job market. *Issues in Labor Statistics.*

Bureau of Labor Statistics. (2010). *Women in the labor force, a databook .* Retrieved March 1, 2012, from BLS Labor Force Statistics from the Current Population Survey, http://www.bls.gov/cps/ wlftable7-2010.htm

California Employment Development Department. (2011, First quarter). *OES Employment & Wages by Occupation Oakland-Fremont-Hayward Metropolitan Division.* Retrieved December 1, 2011, from California Labor Market Information: http://labormarketinfo.edd.ca.gov/

California Employment Development Department. (2011). *Overview of Occupational Employment Statistics (OES) Survey.* Retrieved from OES Survey: http://www.labormarketinfo.edd.ca.gov/ ?pageid=154

California Fair Employment & Housing Commission. (2007). *The Fair Employment and Housing Act.* Retrieved March 1, 2012, from fehc.ca.gov: http://www.fehc.ca.gov/act/default.asp

Carroll, Lewis (1923). *Alices's adventure in Wonderland and through the looking glass .* Chicago, IL: C. Winston.

Center for Adult English Language Acquisition. (n.d.). *FAQs.* Retrieved March 1, 2012, from CAELA.org: http://www.cal.org/caela/esl_resources/faqs.html

Collier, V. P. (1989). How long? A synthesis of research on academic achievement in a second language. *TESOL Quarterly, 23*(3), 509–531.

CPP, Inc. (n.d.). *Strong Interest Inventory.* Retrieved March 1, 2012, from cpp.com: https://www.cpp. com/products/strong/index.aspx

Department of Health & Human Services. (1985). *Competency-based Mainstream English Language Training Resource Package.* Washington, DC: Social Security Administration, Office of Refugee Resettlement.

Deutsch, P. M., & Sawyer, H. W. (1990). *A guide to rehabilitation.* New York: Matthew Bender.

Donnell, C. M., Reyes, S. S., & Porter, D. F. (2004). Examining rehabilitation counselor preparedness as vocational experts. *Journal of Forensic Vocational Analysis, 7*, 35–41.

Eriksen, E. H. (1963). *Childhood and society* (2nd ed.). New York: Norton.

Faberman, R. J. (2011, Q4). *How do businesses recruit?* Retrieved March 1, 2012, from Federal Reserve Bank of Philadelphia Business Review, www.philadephiafed.org/researach-and-data/ publications/business-review/2011/q4

Government Accounting Office. (2005, December). *Older workers: Labor can help employers and employees plan better for the future.* Retrieved March 1, 2012, from gao.gov: http://gao.gov/new. items/d0680.pdf

Havranek, J., Field, T., & Grimes, J. W. (2005). *Vocational assessment: Evaluating employment potential* (4th ed.). Athens, GA: Elliott & Fitzpatrick.

Hipple, S. F. (2010, September). Self-employment in the United States. *Small Business Trends, 3*(9), 17–32.

Hogoboom, W. B., & King, D. B. (2008-2011). *Family Law (The Rutter Group California Practice Guide).* Eagan, MN: Westlaw.

Ilg, R. (2011, May). *How long before the unemployed find jobs or quit looking?* Retrieved March 1, 2012, from BLS Issues in Labor Statistics, Summary 11-01: www.bls.gov/opub/ils/ summary_11_01/unemployed_jobs_quit.htm

International Association of Rehabilitation Professionals. (2007). *IARP Code of Ethics, Standards of Practice and Competencies.* Retrieved March 1, 2012, from rehabpro.org: http://www.rehabpro.org/standards-ethics/12.2007.pdf/view

Jacobsen, J. P., & Levin, L. (1995, September). Effects of intermittent labor force attachment on women's earnings. *Monthly Labor Review, 118*(9), 14-19.

Job Star. (n.d.). *Hidden job market – What is it?* Retrieved March 1, 2012, from Job Star Central, Job Search Guide from your Local Public Library: http://jobstar.org/hidden/hidden.php

Johnson, R. W., Mermin, G., & Resseger, M. (2007). *Employment at older ages and the changing nature of work.* Retrieved March 1, 2012, from AARP Public Policy Institute: http://www.aarp.org/ppi

Jones, E. (2004-05, Winter). Getting back to work: Returning to the labor force after an absence. *Occupational Outlook Quarterly*, pp. 30-42.

Leahy, M. J., Chan, F., Taylor, D., & Wood, C. &. (1998, Jan/Feb). Evolving knowledge and skill factors for practice in private sector rehabilitation. *The Rehabilitation Professional*, 34–43.

Leahy, M. J., Szymanski, E. M., & Linkowski, D. C. (1993). Knowledge importance in rehabilitation counseling. *Rehabilitation Counseling Bulletin, 37*(2), 130–146.

Carroll, L. (1923). Alice's adventures in Wonderland and through the looking glass. Chicago, IL: John C. Winston.

Migration Policy Institute. (2010). *American Community Survey and Census Data on the Foreign Born by State.* Retrieved March 1, 2012, from Migration Policy Institute : http://www.migrationinformation.org/datahub/acscensus.cfm

National Association of Child Care Resource & Referral Agencies. (2010). *Child Care in America 2010 State Fact Sheets.* Retrieved March 1, 2012, from naccrra.org: http://www.naccrra.org/policy/docs/ childcareinamericafactsheet.pdf

Neulicht, A. T., Gann, C., Berg, J. F., & Taylor, R. H. (2007). Labor market search: Utilization of labor market research and employer sampling by vocational experts. *The Rehabilitation Professional, 15*(4), 29–44.

Oxford University Press. (1971). *The Compact Edition of the Oxford English Dictionary.* London, England: Oxford University Press.

PAR, Inc. (n.d.). *About PAR, Inc.* Retrieved March 1, 2012, from PAR, Inc.: http://www4.parinc.com/ About.aspx

Puzella, C. (2000). Earning capacity as a factor to be considered in ordering spousal support. *Journal of Contemporary Legal Issues Part Six, 11*(1), 319.

Robinson, R. (2011). *Identificaton of core variables to be considered in an assessment of vocational earning capacity in a legal-forensic setting: A delphi study (Doctoral dissertation).* Retrieved March 1, 2012, from ProQuest: http://etd.fcla.edu/UF/UFE0043197/robinson_r.pdf

Saxon, J. L. (2008, July). Imputing income to parents in child support proceedings. *UNC Family Law Bulletin, 23*.

Shane, S. (2008, April 28). *Startup failure rates – the REAL numbers.* Retrieved March 1, 2012, from Small Business Trends: www.smallbiztrends.com/2008/04/startup-failure-rates.html

Sleister, S. L. (2000). Separating the wheat from the chaff: The role of the vocational expert in forensic vocational rehabilitation. *Journal of Vocational Rehabilitation, 14*, 119-129.

Social Security Administration. (n.d.). *Age to Receive Full Social Security Retirement Benefits.* Retrieved March 1, 2012, from ssa.gov: http/www.ssa.gov/pubs/retirechart.htm

Titus, S. (2003, June). *Key reasons why small businesses fail.* Retrieved March 1, 2012, from Institute for Independent Business: www.summitbusinesssolutions.ws/docs/reasons_biz_fail.pdf

Toosi, M. (2009, November). Labor force projections to 2018: older workers staying more active. *Monthly Labor Review*.

Tracy, L., & Wallace, A. (2010). The impact of case law on vocational expert examinations in marital dissolution. *The Rehabilitation Professional, 18*(1), 19-20.

Tracy, L., & Wallace, A. (2008, May). The impact of case law on vocational expert exams and opinions in family law. Paper presented at the International Association of Rehabilitation Professionals conference, Los Angeles, CA.

Truthan, J. (2003-2007). *Pocket Guide to the Dictionary of Occupational Titles (DOT).* Spokane Valley, WA: SkillTRAN.

U.S. Equal Employment Opportunity Commission. (2008). *ADA Disability Discrimination.* Retrieved March 1, 2012, from eeoc.gov: http://www.eeoc.gov/laws/types/disability.cfm

Vance, J. (2010). Chaplin at Keystone: The Tramp is born. *Notes for the 4-DVD collection of restored Chaplin films*. London, England: Flicker Alley.

Weed, R., & Field, T. F. (2001). *Rehabilitation consultant's handbook.* Athens, GA: Elliott & Fitzpatrick.

What is collaborative practice. (n.d.). Retrieved March 1, 2012, from International Association of Collaborative Professionals (IACP): http://www.collaborativepractice.com/_WhatIs.asp?M=1&MS=2

World Health Organization. (2001). *International classification of functioning, disability and health.* Geneva, Switzerland: WHO.

[1] The words *work, career, job, occupation, vocation*, and *employment* have nuanced differences, referring variously to difficult tasks, a life plan for employment, a particular opportunity, a grouping of similar jobs, activity done with natural and acquired skills, and paid service. In this book, however, the words will be treated as synonyms and used interchangeably except where noted.

2 This quote is hard to track but may be a paraphrase by psychologist Erik Erikson of a conversation with Freud. Erikson E. H. Childhood and society (2nd ed.), New York: Norton, 1963

[3] *Trier of fact*: the person responsible for making final decisions in a legal case. Family law cases are not decided by juries; in family law, the trier of fact is the judge or commissioner hearing the case. The expert's role is to inform the trier of fact so that the judge's decision is based on expert information. The expert forms conclusions but does not make final decisions about the use of those conclusions.

[4] The ten core knowledge and skill areas: Vocational counseling and consultation services; medical and psychological aspects of disability; individual and group counseling; program evaluation and research; case management and service coordination; family, gender, and multicultural issues; foundations of rehabilitation; workers' compensation; environmental and attitudinal barriers; and assessment.

[5] The Commission on Rehabilitation Counselor Certification (CRCC) is an independent, not-for-profit organization that certifies the professional backgrounds of practitioners in the rehabilitation counseling profession. CRC (Certified Rehabilitation Counselor) and CCRC (Canadian Certified Rehabilitation Counselor) designations indicate a higher level of specialized education and training, a thorough understanding of key competency standards based on current practices in the field, adherence to the Code of Professional Ethics for Rehabilitation Counselors, and an ongoing commitment to continuing education. Accessed 9/2/11 at http://www.crccertification.com

[6] *Pro se* legal representation means advocating on one's own behalf before a court, rather than being represented by a lawyer. This status is sometimes known as *propria persona* (abbreviated to "pro per")

[7] See Appendix E.

[8] I am indebted to the IARP Forensic group for their wisdom and insights into this point.

[9] The Standard Occupational Classification (SOC) system is used by Federal statistical agencies to classify workers into occupational categories.

[10] 'Validity' has many definitions; in this article, 'validity', how well a measure represents what it purports to represent, broadly refers here both to *content validity*: how much the measure covers a representative sample of the domain, and *predictive validity*: the degree to which the measure can predict (or correlate with) with other measures at some time in the future. "Reliability' refers to the ability to repeat the procedure and obtain the same result.

[11] From *In re Marriage of Regnery (CA 1989), 214 Cal.App.3d 1367* the original three prongs of the test that an individual has an earning capacity are: "ability to work," "willingness to work," and "opportunity to work which means an employer who is willing to hire."

[12] Diagnostic and Statistical Manual of Mental Disorders IV is the standard classification of mental disorders used by mental health professionals in the United States. The DSM uses a "multiaxial" system for assessment. This assessment model is designed to provide a comprehensive diagnosis of the entire scope of factors that account for a patient's mental health. There are five axes in the DSM diagnostic system, each relating to a different aspect of a mental disorder: I – acute symptoms; II – personality disorders and developmental disorders; III – medical conditions; IV – psychosocial stressors; V – level of functioning (GAF score 0-100). From psyweb.com accessed at http://www.psyweb.com/DSM_IV/jsp/dsm_iv.jsp

www.ingramcontent.com/pod-product-compliance
Lightning Source LLC
Chambersburg PA
CBHW080613270326
41928CB00016B/3042